WE ARE NOT OKAY

Elegy for a broken America
Memoir-in-essays

CHRISTIAN LIVERMORE

Indie Blu(e) Publishing
Havertown, Pennsylvania

PRAISE FOR WE ARE NOT OKAY

"A moving meditation on American precarity. If, as Baldwin has written, home is an irrevocable condition, *We Are Not Okay* argues that the same might be said for poverty. Livermore is sensitive, insightful and provocative and her book is not to be missed."
—Junot Díaz, Pulitzer Prize-winning author of *The Brief Wondrous Life of Oscar Wao*

"If you're born white trash, do you ever stop feeling that's who and what you are? Christian Livermore's unadorned reflections on "class-passing" are real and raw and nervy. In reading this book, you will see what Americans try to ignore: the damage being done by our class system, which distorts everything it touches. *We Are Not Okay* tells a far more powerful story than J.D. Vance did, in a truly honest voice—which is what's been missing from most modern memoirs."
—Nancy Isenberg, author of *White Trash*

"We are the beneficiaries of Livermore's lack of fucks, of her rejecting the luxury of a rhetoric that presupposes an inherently disordered subject can be treated with writerly order, of her relentless and courageous and entertaining and upsetting display of the effects of poverty. To us, Christian Livermore is saying, "Let me explain something to you," and we need to listen."
—Robert Fromberg, LA Review of Books

"*We Are Not Okay* is a beautifully written, unsettling portrait of the failure of the American Dream. In it, Livermore gives us clearly wrought, moving examples of the ways in which the myth of America-as-meritocracy has crumbled. She deftly

shows us what we already know – that liberty and justice are for the few lucky enough to have inherited them."
—N. West Moss, *Flesh & Blood: Meditations on Infertility, Family, and Creating a Bountiful Life* (Algonquin 2021)

"*We Are Not Okay*, is not fiction, nor indulgent biography, but a polemic against the tyranny of deprivation. Livermore viscerally illustrates at a granular level, why the poor stay poor and how choice plays no significant part in this perpetuation."
—Belinda Roman, PhD, Assistant Professor of Economics at St. Mary's University

"The teetering house on the stark cover of Livermore's book is home for many of us. If I had a house, it might have been my own. This is *We Are Not Okay*'s appeal: it is a book that sends a familiar vibration in all of us (except the wealthy 5%), "us" meaning the lower, working, striving-to-be-middle-class end gamers. I think Livermore (and I) are accurate in our assumption that there are more of us in this category, more of "us" than we want to admit to. It's taken me decades to shrug off my mother's middle class aspirations and acknowledge that we've balanced on that razor edge for generations, a paycheck, a job, a single recession, a whiff of luck and one good friend away from being not okay."
—JoAnn LoSavio, PhD, Assistant Professor of History, Washington State University, Vancouver

For information, address
Indie Blu(e) Publishing
indieblucollective@gmail.com

Print ISBN: 978-1-951724-16-0
eBook ISBN: 978-1-951724-20-7
Library of Congress Control Number: 2022941326
Indie Blu(e) Editorial Team
Candice Louisa Daquin, Primary Editor
Victoria Manzi
Cover Design: Christine E. Ray

For my grandmother Gig, who saved me

ACKNOWLEDGMENTS

I am enormously grateful to Candice Louisa Daquin, Victoria Manzi, Christine E. Ray and everyone at Indie Blu(e), who saw value in what I had written and who said Yes when all I had heard for years was No. I am thankful for the care with which they have treated this manuscript from the moment it entered their hands. Thanks, too, to Candice for her wonderful and sensitive editing of this book. I am grateful for her thoughtful and insightful ideas. The book is better for them.

I am grateful to John Burnside, who encouraged me to write this book and helped me understand that we must write about such experiences so that others who have gone through similar trials will realize they are not alone.

I am also grateful to Jacob Polley, Lesley Glaister and Mai Lin Li for their constant support of my writing and their efforts on my behalf.

Thanks, too, to Iain Maloney and Tess O'Hara for their feedback on an early draft of this manuscript. Their suggestions greatly improved it. Thanks to Iain as well for his support over the last five years. Iain was my very first book editor, and ever since then he has always been very generous and ready to provide guidance and advice about my writing in particular and publishing in general.

I am grateful to *The Texas Review, Salt Hill Journal*, Galley Beggar Press, and *The Undertow Review*, who first printed versions of essays and a story in this volume entitled *Drugs My Mother Took, My Father Died Today, Boys in Masks*, and *All Come to Look for America*, respectively.

Thanks also to my family—my mother, my sisters Jennifer and Charity, my brother Adam, my nieces Lily and Grace and the rest of our mad clan—just for being them, and especially for making me laugh. It's a gift that has made my life rich beyond measure. Sometimes we want to kill each other, more than most families even, but I wouldn't change a thing.

And to Stephen Sacco, whose all-weather friendship, support and cheerleading have made him the rock of my life. Even though he won't admit that he broke my vacuum cleaner.

Some names and incidental details have been changed to protect the identities of those written about in this book.

"Anyone who has ever struggled with poverty knows how extremely expensive it is to be poor."

— James Baldwin

WE ARE NOT OKAY

"Perhaps home is not a place but simply an irrevocable condition."

— James Baldwin, *Giovanni's Room*

I am rummaging through the junk drawer in my father's kitchen, looking for clay, or putty, or caulking. I am twelve years old, and I have an assignment due the following day for Earth Science. I have to make a working volcano. Most of the time there is no mustard, so I don't know how I'm going to find the ingredients for a working volcano. Even now, years later, the bar for financial security is mustard. And paper towels. If I can afford both mustard and paper towels, I feel I'm doing pretty damn well. But on the night in question, my father has said he can't afford the Plaster of Paris I need to make this working volcano, so I'm looking for anything I can use instead.

I call it my father's kitchen. It's my father's apartment, really. I live there, I suppose, but it would be more accurate to say that I occupy the back bedroom of the place. I use the bathroom, and forage food from the kitchen cupboards and refrigerator; cereal and bread and government cheese and whatever else I can find, but mostly I keep to my room and my father keeps to his, lying on his bed listening to Frank Sinatra albums or watching Tarzan movies.

Nobel laureate Amartya Sen tells us that shame lies at the core of poverty. Anyone who grew up poor instinctively knows this to be true. She feels that shame every minute of every day, in the background if she is feeling good, in her face if she is not. The shame I already felt was about to get worse, and it would be ground into my bones forever.

It is early in my seventh-grade year. Until now I have been in class only with students from my side of town, the poor side. But it's a small town, so the rich kids and the poor kids are now funneled into one junior high school, and I find myself sitting next to classmates sporting all the markers of wealth: Straight teeth and sandy hair, Izod T-shirts and madras skirts and boat shoes. My father bought me two new school outfits, from Caldor. A pair of corduroys and a flowered peasant top (for the first day), jeans and a button-down collared shirt that makes me look like a security guard. I am desperate for a pair of boat shoes and have found some at the Salvation Army that are a size too small. I buy them anyway with three dollars I got somewhere, I don't remember where, and I jam my feet into them and wear them until a bony bump emerges on my heel. Eventually I can't take the pain anymore and give up wearing them. The bump is there to this day.

I find nothing in the kitchen, so I move to the bathroom, picking through the mounds of cotton balls and razors underneath the sink. My gaze descends the row of shelves in the bathroom closet, and finally, on the floor, settles on an unopened bag of kitty litter. This is the last place in the apartment. There's nowhere else to look. I take the bag, turn to the sink and remove the plastic top from an empty mouthwash bottle that's been sitting there for months. I gather cleaning supplies, go to my room, and get to work.

I stir the litter into a sluice held together with flour, water and glue until it resembles a melting ice cream sundae. I hollow out a cavity at the top, insert the mouthwash cap and smooth the slurry around it to hold it in place. When it comes time for the volcano to erupt, I will pour a mixture of the cleaning supplies into the mouthwash cap, they will react and overflow like lava. I've tested it. It isn't what I'd hoped to bring in, but it will work.

In class the next day I arrive before anybody else and set my volcano on the windowsill. Bits of kitty litter shake loose onto the tray and I quickly take my seat. My classmates file in and place their exquisitely constructed volcanos alongside it, painted, some snow-capped, with tiny trees dotting the landscape below, some even with miniature villagers who will be swallowed up in the impending eruptions. As they set down their volcanoes they cluster around mine and laugh, and I sit in my seat pretending to be engrossed in a book. The teacher arrives and class begins. One by one my classmates demonstrate their volcanoes, which spew and sputter and send lava flowing down their perfectly crafted slopes.

When we are down to one volcano—mine—Mr. Brown calls on me to take my turn. I picture the volcano behind me, kitty litter pebbles skidding off its sides, and I feel my face bloom red and say I haven't done the assignment. There is only one volcano left, and all the other students have demonstrated theirs, so Mr. Brown knows I'm lying and so do all my classmates, but Mr. Brown is a prince among men and pretends he doesn't. He pretends to scold me for not doing my work and says that just this once, because I'm usually such a good student, he'll give me extra time.

At home I tell my father what happened and give him a note from Mr. Brown. I don't know what it says but I think my father is embarrassed by it. He drives me to the store and buys me Plaster of Paris, and I work all weekend to finish my volcano, and demonstrate it the following Monday.

The shame of this episode is with me even now. It's like a piece of gut I've coughed up into my throat, and it will be there until the day I die.

The more research scientists do on people who grew up in poverty, the more they realize that living in poverty is like being in a war. People who have grown up poor can have PTSD, and many don't have the mental bandwidth that other people have for normal life stressors. Or at least I don't. I become frustrated very easily. If I can't get the lid off a jar, I feel like throwing the thing across the room. I once heard somebody say to an easily frustrated person, "Who do you think you are? Everybody has to deal with these inconveniences. Why do you think you're so special that you don't have to?" They have completely misunderstood, at least if it were me they were talking to. It's that I had already experienced so many normal life stressors by the time I was ten, I used up more than most people deal with in a lifetime. Ironically, that has also left me all out of fucks. I am frustrated and out of patience, so I am ready to dispatch with certain normal life stressors very quickly. I usually do this with the phrase 'Let me explain something to you,' and very calmly and deliberately explain to the person why they had better stop whatever they are doing. It's a strange amalgamation of emotions, and I don't always understand it myself.

Some things never leave you. You carry them forward to the third and fourth generation. Those things can be good, or they can be bad. When James Baldwin wrote the words in *Giovanni's Room* that begin this chapter, he was writing of social isolation, and one of the things he was grappling with was 'passing.' In *Giovanni's Room*, the scholar Valerie Rohy wrote, for Baldwin and millions of black and gay people, 'passing' had to do with racial and sexual identity. For me, passing means something different. It is a highly freighted term for a cis white person to use, I know, but I can think of no other way to describe it. For me, passing means trying to be anything other than what I was, and what I fear so desperately I always will be: poor white trash.

I am leaning against the wall in a game arcade watching another girl play pinball. A group of us are standing around her. The other girls have taken their turns and are waiting for the girl to use up her quarter so they can go again. The ball pings against the sides of the machine and bells trill and lights flash. I am desperate to play, but I don't have any money.

The girls are part of the drum corps I also belong to. We are at Hershey Park in Pennsylvania, on the tail end of a ten-day trip to perform at Disney World. I spent weeks selling candles and chocolate bars to raise money for the trip. That fund-raising covered the cost of gas for the bus and the other travel costs. But it didn't include any spending money. The other kids have received cash from their parents, enough to play arcade games and buy T-shirts and candy and souvenirs. Before I boarded the bus the morning we left, my father gave me $20. I spent it by the end of the third day. I do not belong here.

The girl's quarter shows no signs of giving out. She has kept the same ball in play for about five minutes, bouncing it off the sides, batting it away with the levers whenever it ricochets back. The director of the corps, Mr. Johns, comes up. He watches the game a minute, then looks at the other girls, their quarters ready, then at me. I lean against the wall, trying to look disinterested.

"Don't you want to play?"

"I'm fine."

"Don't you have any money?"

"I had $20, but I spent it."

"Your father gave you $20 for ten days?"

I don't answer. I feel the heat rising on my face. I manage a shrug.

Mr. Johns takes out his wallet and finds a $100 bill and offers it to me. I thank him but decline.

"It's okay," he says. "Take it. I'll get it back from your father."

I know I shouldn't. I think of how angry my father will be that I told. How angry he'll be that he'll have to repay the $100. But I am nine years old and the pinball machine is ringing and the lights are flashing and I want to play. I take the $100 and thank Mr. Johns, and run to the change machine to get quarters.

I know I am lucky to have gone at all. But that's part of the shame. The other kids belonged there. I was lucky to have been included. I am a charity case.

I don't know exactly when I gave up on America. I only know that it was long after America gave up on me. There are many stories of America, but this story is one we don't hear so often. It's the version of ourselves we don't like to think about, the one where poor people can't always pull ourselves up by our bootstraps, where not every smart kid makes it out of the ghetto. The one where the American Dream is a lie. How do I tell it? How do I tell it so you will understand? Not for sympathy, just so you will understand what it has done to us, growing up poor.

John C. Calhoun said, "The two great divisions of society are not the rich and poor, but white and black." With that pronouncement, he told one lie to hide another. He asserted one divide that does not naturally exist and denied one that does. There is no natural division between black and white or brown. Indeed, as James Baldwin and Toni Morrison and Ta-Nehisi Coates and others have pointed out, there is no black or white. The artificial division between black and white was invented by white people in the early days of America's formation through the court system, specifically, by wealthy white people. They needed a reason to justify their right to profit from the labor of others, so they invented labels. Black and white. There absolutely is a division between rich and poor, but the rich would prefer to pretend it doesn't exist. Otherwise, it would be clear that they have taken far more than their fair share and left the rest of us without.

From the outside, I am the story we like to tell ourselves. At the age of 54, by any reasonable standard, I have 'gotten out.' I have a PhD, I've lived in Europe for more than ten years, I was a journalist, I won awards. But on the inside, I am still the little girl in the projects eating government cheese. I dropped out of high school and still managed to get a PhD, but sometimes I don't remember how far I've come. I'm *up here*, but in my mind I'm still *down there*. It's not only that there are external barriers, although there are; I still have severe money problems and have never managed to achieve financial security. The barrier is internal, and it affects nearly everything I do and every interaction I have. I suspect it is the same for many Americans.

People don't want to hear about poor whites for many reasons. One is that it threatens their ability to perpetuate the same old racist narrative that poverty is a 'black problem.' If black people are poor, goes the racist trope, it's because of something they did, so there is nothing society can do about it. If people acknowledge that there are also poor whites, they will have to acknowledge that it is not a 'black' problem. It is a problem with how we reward work, the kind of work we reward most generously, and how we conceive of society's responsibility *for* its poor and not just *to* them—in other words, people are poor because society *makes* them that way and *keeps* them that way, because it is more important to most of America to pay millions of dollars to bankers than it is to pay a decent salary to teachers and sanitation workers and store clerks, and because they need to keep people poor enough to accept work they may not want to do. If people admitted all these things, then they might have to do something about it.

The term *poor white trash* serves the same purpose—to dismiss, to deny, to denigrate. If you're poor, it's because of something you did. If people acknowledge that there are poor whites, they must acknowledge that they themselves could also be poor at any moment—if they think about it, perhaps they already *are*. This threatens the narrative of American exceptionalism, that anybody can get rich in America if they work hard enough. That is not true. It has never been true. But people fervently believe it; some so that they can view their own success as a sign of virtue and the result of their own hard work, others so that they can imagine their struggles as temporary, a bump in the road to their own eventual American Dream.

Contrary to the national narrative, we have always had class in America, and there have always been poor people. The nation was designed that way. As historian Nancy Isenberg, the author of *White Trash: The 400-year Untold History of Class in America*, has written, when the English were establishing colonies in Virginia and New England, they envisioned the poor as an expendable labor pool that would till the soil and husband the animals and build the colonies. They shipped them—the working poor, ex-soldiers, beggars, and criminals—to Jamestown, the Colony of Virginia and the Massachusetts Bay Colony and, in exchange for their passage, they would work to build the New World. They called them 'waste people.'

Nobody wants to hear about poor whites, unless those whites are what people call rednecks and they voted for Donald Trump. I don't know any poor person who is a Republican. All the poor people I know are Democrats. And I mean yellow dog Democrats, an expression which means we would vote for *a ol' yella dog* before we would vote for a Republican. I can only ever recall meeting one poor person who voted for Donald Trump, and he had brain damage from an IED in Iraq. We vote Democrat, that is, when we vote, because we sometimes have trouble getting to polling stations, for lack of transportation, a lack of childcare, an inability to get the time off work, disabilities, and other problems.

We don't have the generational wealth of home ownership that allowed many working-class whites to move up to the middle class. It was also denied to black people because of redlining to keep black people out of 'white neighborhoods,' another way that black people and poor whites are in the same boat. Poor whites are kept out of those white neighborhoods, too, just in different ways; minimum credit scores we can't meet and down payments we can't save up or borrow from family. Another way we are not quite white. We are Catholics, Methodists, Baptists, agnostics, atheists. We are of English heritage and Irish, Italian and Portuguese, German and Polish and French and Greek and Hungarian and Scottish and Dutch.

I grew up in Groton, Connecticut. The way I grew up conflicts with the idea people have of Connecticut as nothing but big houses and leafy neighborhoods and clench-jawed bankers with Brahmin accents, the narrative you see in films, on television and in books. Unlike some working-class communities where factories that had formerly employed a whole town shut down and threw an entire community of working-class people into poverty, Groton had—and still has—two thriving major employers, Pfizer and Electric Boat, which employed a large part of the town and the surrounding towns besides, but no one in my family worked there. Hardly anyone in my family worked at all.

My father blamed a teenage dive off a dock into shallow water for a neck injury and worked less and less until he stopped working altogether and went on welfare. He continued to cut hair in the kitchen and used the money to buy the first VCR as soon as it hit the market, as well as a stereo and every Frank Sinatra tape he could find. When he couldn't pay the rent anymore, he went on welfare and we moved to the projects. My mother had moved herself and my brother Adam there years before, along with my sister Jennifer, who she had after marrying my stepfather. My sister Charity would come along much later, from another man my mother lived with for several years.

The truth is, we couldn't stay where we were. We did not belong in a middle- or working-class neighborhood. It would not allow us to be who we were. So, we moved down, and down, and down again, until we settled in a place where our family's antics would be tolerated by our neighbors because they had no choice. No one had anyplace else to go.

No matter how much we cleaned, the apartment was crawling with cockroaches. One night as I lay awake in bed, I looked up and saw one crawling on the ceiling directly above me. I launched myself out of the bed and slept on the couch that night. The next day I prowled my room with Raid, but I never found that cockroach.

In the projects, every time I went outside, there was a need to be on guard. The scowl, arms at the ready, casual but alert, show that I was watchful, ready to go, that I couldn't be caught unawares, either by a girl who wanted to jump me or a boy who wouldn't accept no. Years before, when I was seven years old, an older boy of about twelve stole our kickball as friends and I played. I went to retrieve it, and he slammed it into my stomach so hard he knocked me to the ground. As I sat on the tar, catching my breath, I heard a voice above me.

"Did you hit my sister?"

I looked up. I don't know why he was there, he didn't even go to that school anymore, but there stood my brother. Adam's reputation preceded him, and the boy began stammering and apologizing.

"Oh, is that your sister? Sorry, man, I didn't know, I wouldn't have—"

But before he could finish the sentence, my brother punched him in the stomach. After that, he taught me to fight. The elbow is the hardest bone in the body. Use it. A hand to the nose will knock somebody out cold, but be careful or you might kill them. If they have hold of you from behind, a headbutt to their face will break their nose.

I also began to realize that I could use things in my environment, so when a school bully picked on my friend on the playground and began shoving her, I tapped him on the shoulder, and when he turned, I knee'd him in the groin, spun him around, and slammed his face into a metal maypole. He later went to prison for rape.

But if you got caught out in the open, you had to front. A girl got in my face in the school parking lot one day out of the blue, throwing arms, her face up in mine. Her breath had that stale quality of someone who didn't brush her teeth regularly. A crowd gathered to watch. I didn't even know what I had done to her. Act casual. Eye the field, see what you can use. But we were in the wide open.

"Look," I said, my voice casual, my arms at my sides, but flexing, ready. "We can go if you want, but I don't want to hurt you. I don't even know what you're mad about."

She fronted a little longer and I held my ground, my heart pounding, that click of dread in my throat. Then I guess she decided I might be able to take her.

"You're all right," she said, offering her hand. "I thought you'd chicken out, but you ain't no punk. You're a good kid."

I shook for an hour afterward.

You become hard. Don't smile. Don't show weakness. That is with me still. I never stroll. Part of me is always on watch, waiting for the unexpected launch, the assault, the confrontation, the male on the hunt. I catch myself doing it and relax my arms, then a little while later I notice I'm clenching again, my shoulders tight. The need to do this is exhausting. The need to hide it even more so, to hide it from friends and colleagues who think I'm another kind of person, that I'm like them, that I'm comfortable in my own skin.

When I talk about poor people, I do not mean working class. It's important to stress that. There are many ways to explain the difference. It is in the shame a poor child feels in the cafeteria line for his free school lunch, in the face of a single mother as she tries to hide her food stamp card from the person behind her in the check-out line, in the worry of a man who has just finished another 12-hour shift and still doesn't know if he'll have enough to buy groceries for his children.

One way to explain it is in a conversation I had recently with a friend. He insisted that, until recently, America was guided, to its benefit, by middle-class values, that there was an understanding that education was important, knowledge was important, that you went to work, did your job, came home, kept your yard clean, respected your neighbors. Poor people do that, too, I said. My grandmother did that. It struck me, then, that we were talking about the same things; we were just using different terminology.

When my friend talks about the middle class, he mostly means the working class. Teachers make $30,000 to $50,000 a year. Teachers are middle class. Garbage collectors make $60,000, but nobody would call a garbage collector middle class. Garbage collectors are working class. My friend was talking about his grandparents. His grandfather was a groundskeeper; his grandmother worked in a ball bearing factory. He wanted to laureate their values, but saying that somebody is working class speaks of a lack of sophistication, so he spoke of middle-class values. The values were the same, but he had grown up absorbing the American idea that the middle class are better than the poor. Nobody ever talks about the values of poor people as though they're a good thing.

Working-class people can, for the most part, keep their lights on. They can at least know that they will be able to buy groceries. They probably are not college educated, but they have steady jobs, jobs they may have had for years, jobs with benefits and a pension, however much they have shriveled in recent years. Or they have been laid off from one of those jobs but they have a skill, and that skill conveys pride. As well it should.

Poor people work two or three jobs, unskilled work that doesn't require a trade. Or they don't have the wherewithal to hold down a job and are on welfare. Their parents were poor and their labor wasn't valued, or they were mentally ill or addicts, and their children imbibed that hopelessness. Maybe they have dropped out of high school. Maybe they have bipolar disorder or schizophrenia. Maybe they have an addiction. Mental illness, substance abuse and poverty can go hand in hand, as they did in my family. Which begets which? It's not always that simple. It is not correct to say that drug use causes mental illness or that all those who are mentally ill are poor by choice; the same is true for those who are disabled. Indeed, in my experience, substance abuse is often done for self-medication. My mother did it, my brother did it, many people in my family did it, because they had undiagnosed mental illnesses and were ignored by the system because they were poor. My mother's bipolar disorder went undiagnosed for years, so she lived with the misery of the depression and the crazed ideas fomented by the mania, and we, her children, lived with the outcomes. That is not my mother's fault. It is the fault of the people who saw her behavior and its results as her own fault, a perception colored by the fact that she was poor, and didn't look past that to recognize that she had a mental illness. Other people are just ignored because they're poor. Waste people.

People may pick up the drug or the bottle, and certainly we are all responsible for our own choices, but what has America offered them instead? The idea that we are waste people is older than the country, and that knowledge that you are not valued by society wears you thin. In the housing project where I grew up, we were a bike ride away from the beach. But nobody I knew from the projects went there. Working class people did. But they had cars. There was no public transportation where I grew up. No bus to the beach from the projects. Or to any place of work, significantly. You needed a car or a bicycle. Most people in the projects didn't have a car, except the drug dealers, and they slept during the day. Hardly anyone had a bike. Maybe they had enough money to give their kids a dollar for the ice cream van, but not enough for a bike, not for their kids and certainly not for themselves. And even if they did, they couldn't conceive of the energy it would take, biking to the beach. It's easier to sit on the porch, fan yourself in the heat and take comfort from an ice cream bar. This is the despair of poverty.

I have never owned a home, and I probably never will. Part of the reason for that is that I have never made enough money to make home ownership an attainable—or practical—goal. There was no down-payment loan available from a parent and I couldn't save the money on my own. I could barely pay my bills. Once, when I was living in New York City, a friend called asking if I wanted to split a summer house in the Hamptons. My share would be $2,000. I desperately wanted to go, to get out of the city, to feel the sea air and hear the marsh grass flutter in the breeze and make smoothies and drink them on the deck, to spend time with my friend, but I didn't have the money. Friends went on expensive holidays, ate at upscale restaurants, lived in apartments in Manhattan; I lived in a studio apartment in a condemned building. I had a degree from a prestigious university. I had a professional job. But I have never been successful at saving money.

That is also a consequence of growing up in poverty: the need for immediate gratification. If I get money, I spend it immediately, as though somebody might take it away from me. Because my whole childhood, people did. When I was nine years old, I had saved about $400 from working in my grandmother's lunch shop. Syl's Food Shop, it was called. It had been serving breakfast and lunch to the workers at Electric Boat for years when my grandmother and aunt bought it from

Syl, and they kept the name because the Electric Boat workers knew it. My mother convinced me to open a joint bank account. She would keep the money safe, she said. My father warned me not to do it, but I was drawn by the lure of the bank account as a connection to my mother. So I did it. When I went to withdraw $20 a month later, the account had been cleaned out. When I was twelve, I had saved up more money from working in my grandmother's shop. This time I was smart. I came home every afternoon and hid the bills in my books. A few dollars in each book. One day when I came home, the books were spilled out all over the floor, splayed open, all the money gone. My brother had found it. When I was in my early twenties, I bought a plane ticket to Italy and was waiting for a check to arrive to use as spending money. They sent it to my mother's house, and she convinced a bank teller to cash it.

So, when I get money, I spend it quickly. Psychologists tell us that people who grew up in poverty have trouble controlling impulses, especially the impulse to buy. Being poor can have a permanent detrimental effect on your decision-making.[1] If I had left the house with a dollar in my pocket, I would have spent it by the time I got home. This decision-making continued into adulthood. I once paid $600 for a set of Calphalon cookware when I was about to take custody of my baby sister, even though I only made $23,000 a year. My reasoning was that I had to have enough pots and pans to make a complete Thanksgiving dinner at all times. It's something I'm working on, and I'm much better than I used to be, but not too long ago I bought a skirt on credit for £175 because I thought I would look cool in it at readings.

---

[1] https://www.apa.org/topics/willpower-poverty-financial.pdf

A few years ago, a friend of mine, in a well-meaning attempt to understand the impoverished diets of poor people, ate a Food Stamp diet for a week. On the last day of the diet, he talked about what he had learned and spoke philosophically about his renewed appreciation of healthy food as he prepared to end his restricted diet with his first good meal of the week: homemade vegetable pizza. He thought about what he had learned as he kneaded the pizza dough. He had already sliced the vegetables, and they sat piled high on the cutting board. While he had the best of intentions, what he said made me sad. He had misunderstood.

In his week of eating like poor people, he had missed two crucial ingredients: fear and shame. While he was looking forward to breaking his fast that night, poor people don't get to do that. They don't get to look forward to the end of impoverishment, to a good meal. My friend would eat a healthy meal that night, and he had known throughout the week that he could stop whenever he wanted, that all he had to do if he missed healthy food was open his refrigerator. Poor people never know when their next good meal will come. They look in the refrigerator on the 25th and maybe they only have enough food for a couple more meals but they don't get paid for a week. And vegetables are expensive. Most poor people can't afford them. All of this causes great shame. Shame that they don't make enough money, shame that they can't give their kids decent food, shame that they must rely on government assistance, shame that they can't afford the restaurant their friends want to go to on Saturday night. That shame never goes away. It is not my friend's fault that he does not know this. He doesn't know it because society does not talk about such things, does not want them talked about. The result is that my friend would never understand how poor people feel—never understand me—and I felt sad and alone.

How do I tell it? How do I tell it so you will understand? Not for sympathy, just so you will understand what it has done to us, growing up poor. Because you have to understand. We are not okay.

When I was about twelve, my dentist told my father I needed braces. I received cleanings only occasionally because it was difficult finding a dentist to accept the meager public assistance reimbursement offered for such a procedure. I sat listening as the dentist told my father the state would not pay for braces and asking if he wanted to pay himself. My father offered to pay him $5 a month. That was my father's offer to everyone he owed money to or wanted something from on credit, $5 a month. The dentist refused, and I didn't get braces.

The thing is, my father could have paid for the braces if he had wanted to. He always had thousands of dollars in the house. He hid it in various places, always in an envelope, behind one of his paintings, behind a drawer of his dresser. I became aware of it because my brother once stole it all. This was before we moved into the projects. Adam was four years older than me and had figured out that it was there, and where.

One day I heard my father scream from his bedroom, "He cleaned me out!" I didn't know what that meant, but my brother did. He was off the couch and out the door in a shot. My father ran out after him and tackled him on the front lawn. His plan was to beat him, but my brother knew a lot of karate by now

19

and was nearly as big as my father and far more muscular, so it turned into a real fight, one my father knew he couldn't win, so he let my brother go.

From then on, I always checked the money, and if my father moved it, I searched for the new hiding place until I found it. I just wanted to know how much was there, the extent to which he was withholding things from me for no good reason than he didn't want to give them to me. Nobody knew where he got the money. He had a friend who we were pretty sure had mob connections and that my father did something through him to earn that money, but we didn't know any more than that.

My father cut hair in the house, but not enough to make that kind of money. He had to hide his income from the state or they would have taken away his government check. From the day Adam stole it all, I checked the envelope. It was replenished very quickly, and there were always thousands of dollars in there. One day I counted it to be sure. There was six thousand dollars. The amount never went down, it always went up. Seven thousand, eight thousand. I would count it and put it back. I did not take any. It felt important not to. I didn't want anything from him. Let his neglect be total. One day when I was fifteen my friends wanted me to go to a movie and get pizza with them but I didn't have any money, so I went into my father's room, removed the top drawer of his dresser and took $20 from the envelope that he had at this time taped to the back of it. I hated myself for it. I felt complicit. *Now he has given me something.*

When I was twelve years old, we moved into the projects. Our ultimate descent was preceded by a prolonged downward spiral. When I was born, we lived in a modest but solidly working-class neighborhood. My father worked, and my mother volunteered for political causes. He was a hairdresser, an expert at the beehive and other sought-after hairstyles of the 1960s and made good money keeping middle-class housewives looking stylish, but my parents hated each other, so my father bought expensive cars and clothes and my mother drank and took drugs and had affairs. Then fashions changed, and my father had no particular talent for the feathered look or the shag, and the money dried up.

My parents divorced when I was seven and my mother gave my father custody of me in exchange for the house, while Adam stayed with her. My father and I moved into the back of his beauty shop. I took baths in an old aluminum rain tub, and my father dragged the tub out the front door of the shop and poured the soapy water down the long parking lot into the street. I picked blackberries from the bushes in the parking lot behind the house to put in my cereal. We moved seven times in the next few years. The second-to-last stop was Colonial Manor, a development of two-story, four-unit brick buildings, projects-lite, but by this time my father had stopped working and gone on welfare, and when a spot opened up in the real projects, we moved in.

There is a terrible assumption about who exactly lives in the projects, and it is both racist and true. The residents of projects are often black and Latino, but it is not because, as so many white people say, they don't want to work. They live there, no matter how hard they work, because society often doesn't let them move up. White people have the natural advantage of their whiteness. The assumption is that if you're white you must have done something really wrong to wind up in the projects. This is both racist and false. We hadn't done anything more wrong to land ourselves in the projects than our black and Latino neighbors, except to be poor, but in America that is sin enough.

My father viewed our descent into the projects as 'reduced circumstances' and maintained a strange combination of haughty airs and complete capitulation. He disdained our neighbors as trash, even though most of them had jobs, while he did not, and yet was happy to accept all charity, and received with unctuous gratitude the deliveries from social workers of government cheese, peanut butter and cereal. The cheese came in a rectangular block of traffic-cone orange, had the consistency of a shellacked eraser, and smelled like sweaty socks. At some point I developed blisters around my mouth and a red, raw crust ringed my lips. My Aunt Barbara used it to persuade my cousins to eat their vegetables.

"Do you want to get blisters around your mouth like Chrissy?"

A school nurse took me to her office one afternoon and explained that it was cheilitis. She explained to me some of the nutrient-rich foods I should try to eat to get rid of it. In other words, I had malnutrition. Soon after, I was called to the principal's office and informed that going forward I would receive free school lunches. My father was pleased. More money saved.

It is worth mentioning that shortly after we moved into the projects, I entered the seventh grade. Class groups were organized into Group 1 (the most academically advanced),

Group 2 (middling academic ability) and Group 3 (poor academic ability). Not one black or brown person was in Group 1, and I know they had to be in that school, because everyone in the projects went to that school. I never saw any of them in the lunchroom, either. In fact, I have absolutely no recollection of seeing a black or brown person during school hours at all (apart from one boy, who I will talk about later).

I can only conclude that the black and brown students were automatically deemed less intelligent than the white students and that the administration organized our patterns of movement so we didn't interact, assuming that all the white people would go home to their nice middle-class houses at the end of the day and never see a black or brown person at all. I have no idea where they spent their school hours, because I never saw any of them at school to ask them, and at home in the projects I kept to myself.

Because my childhood was bifurcated and I had spent the first twelve years of it living in a white working-class neighborhood, I had developed the speech patterns of my neighbors and my parents. Whatever else can be said about my parents, they both spoke grammatically flawless English, and they passed that on to me. So, when I moved into the projects, I spoke in a different way from my black and brown neighbors, who grew up speaking black or Latino vernacular. These are kinds of speech that I have come to love, but at first they were unfamiliar, so I kept to myself.

I never adopted either speech style, although some white people in the projects did. It seemed to me racist somehow, as though white people believed that black and brown people couldn't understand any other speech style, that those white people were unaware of the code switching that black and brown people engage in every day when speaking to white people in order to make themselves more 'palatable' to them, and that by speaking black or Latino vernacular white people were telling black and brown people "I understand that you cannot communicate on my level, so I am going to communicate on yours." For white people who grew up hearing black and Latino vernacular, it was a different story. They spoke that way because that was what they had heard all their lives. For myself, I kept quiet, and I listened.

I loved the way my Latino neighbors switched between English and Spanish in the same sentence, depending on which language expressed their thoughts more succinctly or which word was more pleasing to the ear. I loved and understood the logic of black phrasing; for instance, "What you be doing?" If you think about it, it is more logical than standard English and, according to the rules of English, should be expressed that way. "He walks that way, she talks that way, it be's that way." When I hear it now, it feels like home, but because of the way I grew up I've still got one foot in each world and I don't feel comfortable in either.

However, if you speak standard English you fit more smoothly into white middle-class culture. Inside you don't feel that way, but somebody looking at me from the outside might assume, apart from my clothes, that I'm a middle-class white girl. That devalues black and brown people who have just as much value as I do but they are also devalued because they have different speech styles. For black people this was a style they developed as enslaved people in the American South through contact with white rural Southern dialects (although some linguists think that black vernacular shares so many features

24

with African creole languages around the world that it could have developed on its own, but I am not a linguist so I do not know).

At the same time that my father accepted any state or federal aid he was offered, he kept the house in a state of hospital sterility. He said he got it from his mother, who once got angry at him for trying to break open a coconut in the back yard.

"You'll dent the lawn," she allegedly shouted.

He vacuumed almost daily and stood outside the bathroom while I showered and upon my exit, dashed in with a bucket, mop and sponge.

"You were the cleanest white people in the projects," an old boyfriend said.

This may also sound racist, but it was a comment about us, not our black and Latino neighbors, because we weren't the cleanest people, just the cleanest white people. Since there weren't many other white people in the projects, we didn't have much competition for the title. As long as we didn't toss dirty diapers in a pile on the porch like another white family I knew, we were cleaner.

One night the neighbors had a fight—a screaming, wall-thudding kind of fight—and the woman, Jackie, threw her boyfriend out. Later, at around three a.m., I was awakened by banging on our apartment door. (I don't remember where my father was, but I was home alone.) I looked out the bathroom window and saw a firetruck angled into the parking lot and smoke billowing from Jackie's windows, and a fireman waving me out. Jackie's boyfriend had set the building on fire.

This was life. Once I was pursued home from school by a man in his twenties. I evaded him by slipping in and out of the cul-de-sacs and buildings and by-ways of Colonial Manor and breathed a sigh of relief when I watched him give up and head back the way he had come. I fought and beat to the ground a girl a few years my senior after she jumped me for some reason I never learned. Probably a boy. It was often about a boy. At 13, I had to fight off a boy who had claimed he only wanted to keep me company while I was babysitting but wanted to do a great deal more. I managed to force him out and lock the door and sat trembling on the couch until the grandmother I was babysitting for returned home.

The term *poor white trash* is meant to differentiate *these* white people from other white people, *nice* white people, *real* white people. They can't call us the evil names they call black and Latino people because our skin is white, but we are still 'other.' We don't belong. We are poorer than most white people, even working-class white people, and our poverty threatens these white peoples' confidence in their own value. In an America that keeps most people poor so that a few can stay rich, many white people have a tenuous grip on the middle or working classes themselves, so they need to scorn those whom they perceive as lower to keep themselves from despair.

So, we are trash. They call us this because they can't call us the n-word. And we begin to call ourselves this, because we make the mistake Baldwin cautioned his nephew against in his letter to him, published in *The Fire Next Time*. We *believe* what people say about us. I hope my brothers and sisters of color (for that is what we are, and that is how we must think of each other if we're ever to make real progress against racism, but that is a discussion for another day) will not be offended at my comparison of our two struggles. Theirs is many orders worse than mine. I simply return to this comparison over and over again because it is the only thing I can think of that even comes close to explaining my own experience, because many people of color understand what it feels like to suffer. Not from the random tragedies that befall people indiscriminately but to be disdained, not for something you've done, but for something you can do nothing about: *for who you are.*

The term *poor white trash* is a welcome of sorts from the world. It is meant to limit, from the moment you are born, what you can become. And what you can become is *nothing*, or at least nothing more than what you were born as. You are expected to live and die and do everything in between in a lowly state, and this expectation, if you accept it, ensures it will come to pass.

So, we do to each other things like this: Before my father and I moved into one side of the projects, my mother had already moved into the other side with my brother, sister and step-father. It was Christmas time, and my brother, then fourteen, burst through the door, his face streaming blood, one eye swollen shut, crying. My mother ran to him and asked what happened. A neighbor's apartment had been broken into and the Christmas presents stolen. My brother had already developed a police record, so the neighbor, a grown man, thought he did it, ambushed him on his way home from school and beat him up.

My mother called my stepfather, let's call him Jimmy, at the bar he owned with his father, but couldn't reach him. She left a message and went to tend to my brother.

An hour or two later, there was a knock at the door. It was a local cop my mother and stepfather knew.

"You'd better come out here," he said.

My mother went out to the cul-de-sac. Four or five cruisers were pulled up at odd angles, blue lights flashing, and a ring of cops stood around something in the center my mother couldn't see. As she moved closer, she saw Jimmy, staggering around the middle of the circle, drunk, clutching a crowbar.

"I'll kill him," Jimmy said. "Beat *my* kid? I'll kill the sonofabitch."

The cops held their hands up. "Easy, Jimmy, we've already got him in custody. He's going to be dealt with. Put the crowbar down."

"I'll kill him," Jimmy repeated, crying now. "I'll beat his fucking brains out."

Impotent rage at his inability to protect his stepson, and part of the reason for that inability his being out drinking at the time, all there in the tears in Jimmy's eyes, his bewildered listing from cop to cop, his grip on the crowbar.

My brother lost two teeth in the assault. He was given a plastic denture plate with two false teeth attached to it, paid for by public assistance, but it never fit right. He could click it free with his tongue. He later lost it in a prison fight and was never able to have it replaced.

Many things and many people saved me, passed me from hand to hand so that I am here today rather than in a meth house somewhere, or worse. Things and people that many others as good as me and better were not lucky enough to encounter. The greatest of these was my grandmother, who kept me three or four nights a week and took me to work with her in her restaurant until I started school. Once I entered the first grade, I went to the shop after school let out. Gig showed me the thrill of working and getting money put in my hand for it, the joy of sitting on a rock at the beach and looking up at the clouds and guessing what they looked like. She took me on old lady drives and taught me by example how to be stable and dependable.

But if I had to identify one moment when everything about my expectations of myself and what I could achieve changed, it is this: In third-grade English class, the teacher was calling out words and asking students to come to the blackboard one by one to write them out, then whoever spelled a word correctly had to say what it meant. At first the words were simple and those it would be expected third graders could spell. Then she began calling out more and more difficult words, and finally preposterous ones. When she called out antidisestablishmentarianism, the students all laughed, and Mrs. Sadler smiled and asked if anyone would come to the board and try to spell it. I raised my hand, realizing from the stares of my classmates the moment I had done so that this was foolish, and I grew hot. But Mrs. Sadler, surprised, said, all right, come up and give it a try. I did, and she stared at the word I had scratched out in white chalk on the board, and said that it was correct. She shook her head.

"So then," she said, "what does it mean?"

"I have no idea," I said.

My classmates laughed again, and Mrs. Sadler laughed, too, but she looked at me strangely, with a frown, not disapproving, but, what? Curious?

It was then I became aware of something I could lever to get out, to escape. It wasn't mine. I couldn't claim it. But I could use it. At recess I went to the library and got down a dictionary from the wooden shelves and looked up antidisestablishmentarianism and copied out the definition into my notebook.

The following year I was placed in a program called Gifted and Talented. We studied Spanish and did science experiments and visited the co-creator of Howdy Doody, who lived nearby. For reasons that I still don't fully understand, while many people around me took drugs and drank and settled into lives of insecure work or welfare or prison, I excelled in school.

When I could get there. Because at home I deteriorated. My father, our life, became an anvil weighing me down. I couldn't sleep nights. I lay awake until four, five, six am, and when the alarm went off at seven, I slept through it. One year I missed more than 100 days of school. When I was sixteen, I could endure my father's roof no longer and moved out. He kicked me out, actually. I took a part-time job to pay rent. School and work became too much, and I dropped out.

But I never intended that this would be the end of my schooling, just the end of high school. There were no books in my father's house. There were books in my mother's, but I was not allowed to see her from the ages of 7 to about 12, maybe a bit younger but it's difficult to remember exactly, so I would not discover these books until then. In the meantime, while my grandmother had no books, she told stories. She was a gifted storyteller, and she could turn anything into a story: One day we passed a well in somebody's back yard. "Oh, let me tell you about that well," she said, and she made up some story about fairies living at the bottom of it. She also gave me money every time the RIF truck was coming through. She was very poor, and barely had money for groceries, but she always had a few dollars for the RIF truck.

Reading Is Fundamental is the largest children's literacy program in the United States, and every few months they sent trucks around to schools. They would lay the books out on a long line of tables from the lunchroom, and we could go along and pick out the books we wanted. And they were cheap. At this time, in the mid- to late 1970s, you could buy a book for between 50 cents and a dollar.

My grandmother had been forced by her parents to drop out of school in the eighth grade to work in the family bakery. Her music teacher went to the house to beg her parents to let her continue, told them that she was already a great piano player and could play professionally if she continued with her training, but they were unmoved. My grandmother worked for her father, then got married to a man who turned out to be an alcoholic. She kicked him out and worked three jobs to keep the house payments up and take care of her three children, one of them my mother. She cleaned house for a state Supreme Court judge, she did people's laundry, and she sold Avon. Later she managed to save up enough money to buy Syl's Food Shop with my Aunt Rose. I worked there starting at the age of four. One day my aunt nearly cut her finger off using the meat slicer, and from that day forward she would never use it again. So, it became my responsibility. I was seven years old. That is the thing about poor families. Things need to be done, and many of them are things a child should not be doing, but nobody can afford to hire help, so the children in the family are put to work. My grandmother ran the restaurant until she was too old to work anymore.

Maybe it is that life that she did not choose but which was forced upon her that led Gig to value education and to nurture my love of reading. I do not know. But I am grateful beyond measure. Without my grandmother I really don't know what my life would be, or if I would be here at all.

With this love of books and learning that Gig had given me, after I dropped out of high school, I waited for my class to graduate so I could take the GED and apply for college.

In the meantime, I worked. When I dropped out of school, I got a job at a musical theater company, and my father gave me his old 1976 VW bus to use so I could get to and from work. It had no heat—they didn't in those days—and I used the same kerosene heater my father placed in the well behind the front seats to keep warm, the one my brother propped his feet up on when he was 16 and set his pants on fire. You had to keep the windows cracked so you didn't pass out from the fumes.

One day the bus died. My father had built up excellent credit paying his $5 a month, so he co-signed a car loan, and I bought a used 1984 Subaru. It leaked water into the back seat when it rained, and the water pooled on the floor. The dealership wouldn't fix it, and I didn't have the money to get it fixed, so I lived with it. When I had passengers in the back seat, they had to cross their legs on the seat or prop their knees up on the backs of the front seats to keep them out of the water.

I work for the musical theater company for one season, and then in October, they lay everybody off for the winter. My father screams that I won't be able to make the car payments, that I will ruin his credit. I will have unemployment coming in until the next season starts up, I tell him, and I need the car to go around and apply for other jobs until then. I go to sleep. In the morning, I go downstairs for cereal and look out the window into the parking lot. My car is gone. My father has called the repo company in the middle of the night and had them repossess it. I am 17. My credit is ruined. (I often find myself writing in the present tense in this book. I think it is because these events are always 'now.' I will dream about them when I go to sleep tonight, and I will think about them when I wake up in the morning.)

For a while I survive on unemployment and try to think about how to get another car in time for the musical theater company's second season. In February, I get word that the company will not be reopening. They are going out of business. Now I need a car to apply for jobs and drive to one when I get one. I watch the classified ads. I see an ad for a *1968 Ford Rambler, $1,500. I don't have the money. I get rides to the mall with my friend Alex and fill out job applications. I keep watching the classified ads. The Rambler is advertised the next week for $1,200. The week after that it is $1,000. It goes on this way until finally I see an ad that says "All right, dammit, 75 bucks." I spend the last of my savings from the musical theater job to buy the car.

I get a job at Mrs. Field's cookies in the mall two towns over. I have no money left for the registration and insurance, but I have to go to work to get the money for those things. So, I take the back roads, hopping onto the highway at the last possible moment before crossing the bridge, then back onto the surface roads to the mall. This works for a little while. I nearly have enough saved for the registration and insurance. Then, on my way to work one afternoon, a cop pulls me over next to my old elementary school. He wants to know why I don't have registration or insurance. I explain that I can't afford them and that I have nearly saved enough and that I just need another week or so, but he is unmoved. He makes me get out and lock the car. I ask him if he can give me a ride to work so I don't get fired. He says no. I walk home and call in to work. The manager calls me back. I am fired.

I get a job as a telemarketer. It's an evening job so I won't oversleep, won't get fired. I am driving home one day and the Rambler stalls in traffic. I can't get it started again. The man behind me helps me push the car into the breakdown lane. I have saved enough money to get registration and insurance but not enough to get AAA, and I have no money for a cab even if I were near a phone booth to call one. I leave the car in the breakdown lane and walk home. I call in to the telemarketers. Luckily I am not fired, but I am going to have to get the car back in working order soon or I will not be able to go to work the next day and then I probably will be fired. I call my mother.

"Mom, my car broke down."

"Well, what's wrong with it?"

"I don't know."

"Go see good-to-go Jay."

"Who?"

"Good-to-Go Jay. He's a drunk but he can fix anything as long as you catch him sober."

It was a common story at this time. Good-to-Go Jay was a Vietnam vet. The war had done terrible things to him, so he took up the bottle and couldn't keep a steady job, but the government had gotten what they needed from him so they were content to let him waste away. Waste people.

My mother instructs me to come pick her up, so I call my cousin Susan to come get me and we go pick up my mother. She directs us to the frontage road along the river behind the buildings on Bank Street in New London, where she lives.

"Honk the horn," she says to Susan.

"What?" Susan says.

"He lives on that boat out there." She points to a battered old boat anchored offshore. "That's how you get him, you have to honk the horn."

"He doesn't have a phone?"

"Of course he doesn't have a phone, he lives on a boat illegally anchored offshore. Will you just honk the horn?"

So Susan honks the horn, and we wait.

"Honk it again."

She does. A moment later, a post-madness King Lear-like figure stumbles out from below deck. He has ginger hair and a long scraggly beard and his hair is swimming in matted curls all around his head. He looks toward our car, sees my mother waving and waves back, then begins shuffling around the deck.

"What's he doing?" I ask.

"He's coming in."

The man climbs into a little dinghy, and we wait while he rows in. When he reaches the shore, he ties up, climbs a piling and hoists himself into the parking lot where we are parked. He is hung over but sober. My mother introduces us all and explains the situation to Good-to-Go Jay.

"Well, take me to her and let's see what the problem is."

He climbs into the back seat, and Susan drives back over the bridge to Groton and the street where I left my car in the breakdown lane.

"Yep, there's your problem right there," Good-to-Go Jay says, and he points to something he says is a butterfly clip. "It ain't opening right, so when you stop the car or stall out, it probably ain't gonna start again. Don't worry, that's an easy fix."

He instructs Susan to drive us to the auto parts store on the main shopping street in town, what locals call Burger Mile. He goes into the store and comes out a few minutes later with a box. We drive back to the car, and Jay fixes it right there in the breakdown lane. He climbs into the driver's seat, turns the key and the car starts right up. He looks at me and grins. He charges $25, which my mother pays. Luckily, she had just gotten her government check.

While I am working and dealing with car breakdowns, I am also considering colleges. I knew I would only have enough money to make application at one school, and I decided I wanted to go to New York University. I visited my former guidance counselor for advice on the application.

"Don't bother," he told me. "You'll never get in."

The best I could hope for given my background, he said, was the state university.

Given my background. I don't know what he meant, but I know what I heard. *Because you're poor white trash.* It's very possible he only meant that dropping out of school would be counted irrevocably against me, but with the instinct that had

37

already become ingrained in me, I imagined he saw deep inside me, past my test scores and my polished speech and my careful posture, all the things I had cultivated to convince people—to convince myself—that I had some value, and saw the poor white trash within.

I ignored his advice and applied. One May day when I was nineteen, I went to the mailbox and drew out a large white envelope with a purple torch embossed above the return address. I'd been accepted to NYU. I jumped into my car and drove to the high school to see the guidance counselor, but he was out that day. I made the secretary take a copy of the acceptance letter.

"Leave that on his desk," I said.

I worked all summer, and in September I sold my bicycle, my collection of Archie comics and the typewriter I had been using to write plays. I left my Rambler in my father's parking space in front of our building, and I bought a train ticket to New York. I was getting *out*.

William Winter, a former governor of Mississippi, said, "The only road out of poverty runs past the schoolhouse door." That is true. But what it doesn't make clear is that when you leave the schoolhouse, you might still be dragging the poverty behind you.

At NYU I read Shakespeare and Beckett and Martin Buber and *The Federalist Papers*. I registered for a philosophy class but dropped it after two weeks. I simply did not have the interest necessary to focus on the abstract thinking involved in philosophy. I grew up having to focus on concrete things, like will there be dinner. I had no time for abstract thinking, so maybe I developed a disdain or impatience for it. Right or wrong, maybe I felt it was only something middle-class and rich people had time for. Often I had no money, so my boyfriend shared a meal with me from his meal plan, usually a knish cut in half because potato could keep you fuller longer.

I went to jazz clubs where you could sit and listen to music all night long for the price of one drink and saw Dizzy Gillespie and Ellis Marsalis. I ate at restaurants in Soho and on the Upper West Side and engaged in and overheard self-consciously sophisticated conversations. But every time I entered a place above my station, I imagined a silent poor white trash alarm blaring, alerting people to my presence, them looking at me and thinking, What's *she* doing here?

My friends couldn't see it. Couldn't hear the poor white trash alarm, didn't see what I saw.

"No, you grew up in Virginia," a friend joked. "On your granddaddy's horse farm. With staff."

My friends just saw me, and for that I felt grateful, but also lonely. I didn't belong, I felt it in my bones, and I didn't know how to tell them that.

I visited home about once a month, and everything I had spent the previous weeks pretending didn't exist was all around me again. During one visit my mother slapped me and I pushed her into an easy chair and jumped backwards and up onto the couch, like a cat, my startle reflex still sharp. On another trip we went to visit my brother in prison. I don't remember what he was in for at that time. While we waited, two prisoners who tended the garden started talking to me and tried to get my phone number. When we told Adam about it, he said they were doing life for murder. When I left on Sunday nights, as I sat on the train back to the city, I always felt like I'd forgotten something, left something behind, but I could never figure out what it was.

Slowly, when I have money, I have been having Good-to-go Jay do work on my Rambler. It is now in pretty good working condition. I love the car. I come home for Thanksgiving. I have made plans to drive to my friend Alex's house. I get in a cab at the train station and have him take me to the projects, but when we pull in, I see that my Rambler is gone. There is a rule, my father says when I go inside and ask what the hell happened to my car, that a car can't be left abandoned. They called him and told him to move it. He didn't tell them, it's not abandoned, it belongs to my daughter who is away at college. He didn't tell them, she loves that car and put all her free money into fixing it up. He didn't tell them, she will need it when she comes home for the summer and gets a summer job. "Okay," he told them, and he called a junkyard and had them tow the car away.

After graduation I started working and eventually, after many lost jobs, which I will discuss later in the book, I found work as a copy editor for an ad agency and wrote on the weekends. For a long time, I engaged in class-passing. Because that's what it feels like. That's what it will always feel like, I fear, to have come from where I come from and try to move amongst your betters, which is what they feel like to me, even now. People who come from more privileged backgrounds, middle-class people, even working-class people. To be poor white trash is to be something entirely *other*. I didn't claim to have come from money, but I didn't talk about my background.

Like George Washington, I studied rules of etiquette. How to eat at an upscale restaurant. Work your way through the cutlery from the outside in, the larger glass is for red wine, the smaller for white. I convinced myself that no poor white trash alarm sounded when I entered nice restaurants and that, while I remembered my childhood, it no longer had a hold over me. I was educated and well fed and had money to spend. I had made it out.

One weekend after I'd lived in the city for many years, I went home for a visit. The high rises fell away and the landscape flattened out, and two hours later the train was skirting the shoreline. Soon I could smell rockweed and the froggy mud of the marsh. The train crossed a railroad bridge and the buildings closed in again as we entered the decaying city where my mother still lived. We pulled into the station, and I alighted on the platform and walked the half-mile into the bad neighborhood and to my mother's apartment. My mother at this time lived on the top floor of a two-story house. My sister Jennifer lived downstairs. When I arrived, a bundle of orange and yellow extension cords trailed from my sister's door along the hall and upstairs into my mother's apartment. Her electricity had been disconnected again, as it often was, and she was hooked up to Jennifer's power.

The following afternoon Jennifer asked me to babysit her kids. Jennifer took her purse and keys, and at the door she stopped.

"If a guy called Country comes by, don't let him in. He owes me money and he can't have his stuff back until he pays me."

Country was the latest in a long line of friends down on their luck who my sister had allowed to stay with her for very little money. Jennifer has a big heart and a soft spot for anybody who needs help. More than once she bought groceries for people she knew were struggling to feed their kids, even though she could ill afford it. Several times she bought them for me.

Jennifer had trouble covering the costs of childcare so she could go to her job as a waitress in a pizza place downtown. If a friend needed a place to stay, she provided room and board for a small charge, usually $100 a month, and in exchange, the idea was, the friend would babysit while Jennifer worked. But what happened more often than not was that the friend would eat Jennifer's food, run up her electric bill, disappear whenever it was time to babysit, and sooner or later, move out while Jennifer was away from the house.

This was apparently what Country had done, or my sister had kicked him out. I didn't ask. The longer I was away from that life, the less patience I had for its intricacies. These arrangements felt seedy. Desperate. They *were* desperate, and had I been less anxious to divorce myself from that world, to forget the depredations of my own past, I would have been more sympathetic to the desperation that led to such predicaments because, without the luck I had been graced with, I would be in the same boat and making the same desperate arrangements. As it was, the less I knew, the happier I was. I would be going back to the city soon, to my job in advertising and Sunday brunch on the Upper West Side. This was nothing to do with me.

Not long after my sister left, Country turned up. Just as my sister had instructed me, I told him he couldn't come in. I stood in the door with my hands on the frame.

"I just need to get my records," he said, ducking beneath my arm into the house.

Apparently, his records were in the cellar. He padded down the basement steps, and I heard boxes scraping concrete and things shifting about.

I ran to the kitchen and took the cordless phone from its cradle on the wall. "If you don't leave right now, I'm calling 911."

"I'll just be a sec."

That made me angry. Made me feel like poor white trash again. I didn't even have control over my own space. I told somebody to leave and they refused, ignored me as though I hadn't even said anything.

So I called the police and waited for them to arrive.

Then Country, a box in his arms, began climbing the basement steps. Now I was angry. I didn't want him to come in to begin with, but now that he had and I'd called the police, I didn't want him to leave before they arrived. I wanted him punished. So I locked the basement door. From the other side, Country knocked.

"Hey, let me out."

I leaned against the door jam, phone in hand, and waited.

He knocked again. "Come on."

I felt a breeze on my legs and looked down to see Country's arm protruding through the cat door. (Why there was a cat door to the basement is something I'm not clear about.) I jumped away. I stared stupidly. Having got his arm through up to the elbow, he then poked his head through. It was like the scene in *Alien* where the tiny alien baby rips its way out of John Hurt's stomach.

"Come on, let me out."

I took a few steps back. Country's head was unnaturally pinned to his shoulder because of the tight space through which he had tried to squeeze himself. He twisted and turned, trying to fit the rest of his body through the cat door. Well, what else could I do? I started laughing. Eventually he realized he wasn't going to be able to squeeze his whole body through, so he began flailing his arm, trying to reach the door handle and turn the lock. That made me laugh harder.

"Man, shit," he said.

Apparently realizing he wasn't going to be able to unlock the door or squeeze through the cat door, he tried to pull his head and arm back out. He pulled, then stopped to catch his breath, and pulled again, but couldn't budge. He was stuck. He let out a heavy sigh and his arm fell limp. That sent me into hysterics.

"This shit ain't funny. Come on."

Now I was in a doubly bad position. I had locked him in the basement and I was laughing at him for getting stuck. I definitely couldn't let him out at this point. Who knows what he might do? But as I stood looking down at him, a defeated arm and head hanging limply from a cat door in a house where he was no longer welcome and couldn't even collect his records without the authorities being summoned, I began to feel guilty. I didn't know what mischance had befallen Country that forced him to seek temporary shelter with my sister, but it can't have been pleasant. Now he was stuck in a cat door and a stranger was laughing at him.

I didn't have to worry long about how to rectify the situation because at that point the police showed up. They entered the kitchen, looked at me expectantly, then clocked that a head and arm were protruding from the cat door. They stepped up to him, stopped, studied him a moment, and then they started laughing, too.

"Country, what are you doing, man?"

Apparently this was not Country's first encounter with the police.

"I just came to get my records, and she locked me in the basement."

"Is this your house?"

"No."

"What's the matter with you? You can't just walk into other people's houses."

"She said I could."

"Oh yeah, she said you could. That's why she called the cops and you're locked in a basement with your head stuck in a cat door."

Then they laughed at him some more. Eventually they opened the door, pulled him free from the other side and took him away in the cruiser.

It is many years since I called the police on Country. The different paths of my family's lives have distanced me from my brother and the older of my two sisters. It is in the way we talk, it is in the stories we tell, it is in Country, stuck in a cat door, forced to wait to be hauled away by police. And it is in my guilt, at having called the police on him, at having got out, at having left my siblings behind.

I search for commonalities with them, things we can talk about and share, but because our worlds are so different this has its limits.

"That bitch better step off," Jennifer said one day. "She was talking shit, saying you do this, you do that, whatever-whatever—"

"What does that mean," I said, "whatever-whatever?"

"It means whatever."

"Then why not just say whatever?"

"Fuck off."

My brother tells of a prison stint in which his cell was directly across from a man called John who was known as the Lovers Lane Serial Killer. I haven't been able to find a record of this man, and Adam tends to exaggerate, but this is the story he tells.

John's mouth always hung slightly open, his tongue protruding, and all day long from lights up to lights out, he shuffled back and forth between the bars of his cell and the window. When he got to the bars he would stare across at Adam for a moment, his mouth hanging open, then he would turn and shuffle back, and when he got to the window, he would yell out into the yard, "Twenty-nine cents an hour!" which was the pay for prison labor at that time. He did this every day Adam knew him, except during the 1984 presidential campaign, when on reaching the window he would yell, "Let's hear it for Mondale!"

I love my siblings' stories and wish I could tell ones as good, but I don't want to live the life I would have to live in order to have such stories. Saying that makes me feel guilty too, because it shows that I am setting myself at a distance from my siblings, above them, actually, and I'm ashamed of that.

I don't know what happened to Country. I never asked my sister at the time, and when I asked her about the incident recently, she only vaguely remembered ever having a friend called Country. I find that very sad. That this boy had made such little impression on a friend with whom he had sought shelter. That the world we grew up in made those outcomes often inevitable. That people came and went according to their usefulness and both your needs. Still, added up, Jennifer has more friends than I do. My friends would not get on with them, surely, but Jennifer does. She knows who she is. We can never know what someone else's interior life is like, but whatever she is, she is *that*. I keep most people at arm's length. I don't know how much of me is still pretending to be something else and how much of other people pretending they like me is just courtesy. I worry that, when they look at me, what they're really thinking is, *poor white trash*.

Whenever I prepare to leave at the end of a visit home, I feel a strange longing. I would call it wistfulness, but I'm not sure you can feel wistful for something you never had. It is more a sense of *hiraeth*, a Welsh word that means, according to Samantha Kielar, a longing 'for a home that you cannot return to, no longer exists, or maybe never was.' Because what I longed for was my childhood. Not the one I had, but the one I'd wanted.

When the police took Country away that day, instead of relief, I felt depressed, and for the rest of the weekend I was moody and distracted. On Sunday evening, as the train retraced its route back to the city, I stared out the window at the marshy inlets, their water gone black in the twilight. It hadn't been wrong to call the police, had it? My sister told me not to let him in, and he'd come in anyway. But he'd got what he came for and was leaving, so why didn't I just let him go? I'd wanted to punish him, but that was the first time I'd ever laid eyes on him. What did I care if some kid, barely twenty, was anxious enough to have his records that he'd ignored my admonition not to come in? What I'd really wanted to do was strike some kind of blow, not against Country, against a world in which that kind of thing happened, against the world in which I'd grown up and was trying so desperately to escape, the world Country reminded me of.

I didn't realize this at the time, or for many years afterward. I thought of Country from time to time, and always flushed when I recalled what I'd done, but I didn't know why. It is only now that I realize. It wasn't anger I'd felt but shame, and not at Country. He had done nothing to earn my anger, or my disdain. He was simply a kid from the slums trying to get by, hoping to salvage something he loved in a world that had probably taken from him his entire life, and, stuck there in that cat door, being laughed at by some total stranger, a girl in a madras skirt with her hair pinned up just so, he must have felt utterly worthless. Poor boy. That's when I knew. What I was really ashamed of, still, after all this time, was myself. After all these years, I'm still just the girl with the kitty litter volcano. I don't know if that ever goes away.

I don't class-pass anymore. I wear the clothes I like without regard to fashion or cost. I rest my elbows on the dinner table because I'm in my fifties and my back hurts. After NYU I got a PhD from one of the most prestigious universities in the world and I've earned the right.

But. *But.*

I still feel the difference between me and other people. To one degree or another, it is always with you. Sometimes you don't notice at all and think it's gone. At other times it eats at you, like an infection. Every rejection, every careless remark becomes something more, becomes a verdict on your value. I watch the ease with which some people move through a room, how comfortable they are in their own skins, how confident they are that people want to hear whatever it is they feel like saying. I don't have that. Sometimes it comes from money

49

(though I realize rich people have problems of their own and may be just as uncomfortable in their own skins because of them). Not even a lot of money, just enough so that you have never felt you were imposing. Never felt you were taking up space somebody else deserved more. It comes from not being poor white trash. All these years later I am still seeking the grace to understand what that means, still learning how to move among people comfortably, to be myself and not some impersonation of someone who was, but is no longer, poor white trash.

DRUGS MY MOTHER TOOK

"I think we are well advised to keep on nodding terms with the people we used to be, whether we find them attractive company or not. Otherwise they turn up unannounced and surprise us, come hammering on the mind's door at 4 A.M. of a bad night and demand to know who deserted them, who betrayed them, who is going to make amends."

— Joan Didion, *Slouching Towards Bethlehem*

My mother believes that Vicks VapoRub killed my grandmother. The label reads, 'For external use only.' My grandmother applied it to the insides of her nostrils every night to clear her sinuses, and sure enough, fifty years later she was dead. Because the doctors could never provide any cause of death for my grandmother beyond noting that she smoked for sixty years and she was old, my mother can persist in this half-serious belief and challenge all comers to prove her wrong.

My mother also developed an obsession with necrotizing fasciitis. When my youngest sister was about five, my mother began to besiege first Charity and then her adult children over the slightest injuries. When Charity came home with a scrape on her knee from a fall on the sidewalk, my mother cleaned it and applied iodine until Charity kicked her. When I opened a tiny cut on my hand, so miniscule that I didn't even notice it had happened until she pointed it out, she harassed me all afternoon to clean it out.

"It's going to get infected," she said. "Then before you know it—ut—there's the flesh-eating virus and they'll chop your arm off."

It's ironic that my mother should be so fixated on the various implausible, one-in-a-million scenarios through which a person might die, as for many years she took drugs and drank to a degree that could have killed her. It's a wonder she survived. The obsession with necrotizing fasciitis was probably just a mutated form of her addiction. Having denied herself drugs and alcohol, the obsession and compulsion that were most likely part and parcel of her disease simply found something new to fixate on.

My mother is not terribly helpful at filling in the blanks of her drug use, the details my siblings and I don't know about what, precisely, she did. It isn't that she doesn't want to talk about these things. Whether it is her way of honoring steps four and five of her recovery program (4. Make a searching and fearless moral inventory of ourselves and 5. Admit to God, to ourselves and to another human being the exact nature of our wrongs) or whether it is the attention that accrues to her in doing so, she rather delights in talking about them. It is simply that she can't remember it all. When I ask about those years, she tells me unconnected anecdotes about this or that drug- or alcohol-induced event. My first instinct was to write pointless anecdotes, but that is not true, and also not what I mean. Her stories are not pointless. They are her stories. What I mean to get at is that they lack a point, a 'the-moral-of-this-story-is,' the kind of ending one expects from the well-made play we are often conditioned to expect from stories.

One of her stories involves a drinking friend of hers and the man with whom she was having an affair at the time. I will call them Gail and John.

"Gail and I were drinking on Warner Street on that little porch outside in the back. I was wearing a dress that I made for myself, a purple tunic. So, Gail and I were drinking, and I told John I couldn't see him that night. I think I told him I had cancer or something. Then we were in the kitchen, and I had a bottle, and we kept hearing noises. Finally Gail went and looked, and when she opened the door John fell into the kitchen. He'd been kneeling there at the door listening."

We lived for most of my mother's active addict years, or at least the ones I can remember, in a one-story, olive-green house on a dead-end street, in a modest but aspirationally middle-class neighborhood. This was a climb up from my mother's even more modest childhood, during which my grandmother worked three jobs to feed my mother and two other children. She was seventeen when she married my father; he was thirty-three. She was twenty when my brother was born, and at twenty-four she had me. She must have felt out of place on Warner Street to begin with, out of place in this life, as a mother expected to tend to two children, be a wife to a man nearly old enough to be her father. My father came home the first night of their married life and, smelling nothing cooking, asked her, "Where's dinner?" Beats me, my mother thought. On top of all this, my father was cold and angry, with a vicious temper and an uncurious mind. The angrier he got, the more she used. The more she used, the angrier he got. It must have been daunting for her to try to look normal for the neighbors when half the time she was listing to the right as she walked.

As he got angrier, she looked elsewhere for solace, and began to have affairs. One of the things she says she realizes now is that she didn't know how to live. Everything she learned about life, she says, she learned from reading.

"I was having an affair, and all the people I read about in books, when they had affairs, they always wore nightgowns. So when John came to visit me on Friday night, I always wore a nightgown. He finally said to me one night, 'Don't you have any clothes?'"

She took cocaine and Quaaludes and acid, painkillers and black beauties. ("I don't know what they are, but I did them.") She also liked fermented fruit, and in desperate times would drink vanilla extract. But her drug of choice was speed, "in all its forms." She took handfuls of pills, all mixed up. She got them from a local doctor who ran a pain clinic in Jewett City, Connecticut, a tiny borough of a couple thousand people that used to be home to corn, grist, cotton, and sawmills, but at this time was a scattering of tumbledown homes, bars, and Friday-night polka. Let's say the doctor was called Ridgeland.

You had to go down back roads and over the railroad tracks into the woods to get to his office. Dr. Ridgeland had lawn chairs in the waiting room and had decorated the walls with pages torn out of National Geographic. One day he called my mother in, and in his office were bookshelves lined with huge mayonnaise jars, like the kinds restaurants buy, filled with every color pill imaginable. He was very weak, probably from taking the same pills he doled out to the addicts who visited his office. He would try to pump up the blood pressure cuff, and it would slide down my mother's arm. He would try to slide it back up again, and it would slide back down again, until finally he said, "The hell with it." While this all was happening, other people waiting were opening the mayonnaise jars and taking out pills by the handful.

She also smoked marijuana, though was put off it when somebody gave her a joint laced with something that made her homicidal. She went out on the porch so she didn't kill my brother and me. Then she thought, "That's stupid. I could still go inside and kill you." So she got in her car and drove down to Gail's house. She had left my brother and me alone, but she thought that was better than killing us. Even now she cries talking about it.

"I tried to do the best I could to protect you kids, even from me. When I think of the hell I went through having to make these value decisions. Which is worse? Stay in my house and kill my kids because I'm so fucking crazy, or go to Gail's where I might kill myself on the way but at least you kids would be okay?... Then I started thinking, maybe I'll kill Gail."

As with so many of these stories, she doesn't remember what happened next. In this case, she remembers only that it was okay to go home after a while.

Another story involves the time she got kicked out of Boston. She'd been on her way to pick up grinders. She and the woman she worked for, who owned a shop in the next town over from us, told everyone they were going on a business trip, but the truth was that they had been dealing with a supplier for the business there who they knew only through phone conversations. He had a nice voice, and because of this, they thought he might be good-looking, so they thought they should go there and check him out.

They were staying in an apartment (she doesn't remember whose) and they didn't have a key (she doesn't remember why), so they had to ring all the bells until someone buzzed them in. One night, after mixing tequila and Quaaludes in the bathroom of a local McDonald's, they drove in my mother's big white Cadillac up Commonwealth Avenue near the Museum of Fine Arts (she thinks). Her memories are a strange mix of vivid details and blurry images. She didn't know that the lanes on this road switched directions at a certain time of night, and they were pulled over by police. The officer ran her plates and discovered that she had a large number of outstanding tickets. The next thing she remembers is that she and her friend were escorted to the city limits and told charges would not be pressed if she never returned. She has not been back to Boston since.

"I'm sure they wouldn't remember me now," she said, "but I won't go back because my feelings are hurt."

These stories are part of how we relate in our family. "You remember the time Mom did X?" "You remember the time you did Y?" We probably also tell them the way soldiers tell war stories, turning over and over the details of this or that incident, wondering how we survived. There is a very particular story we tell in my family to try to explain to outsiders how it was; a kind of shorthand for the kind of family we are, and we always laugh when we tell it, because whatever else it is, it's funny.

One night my mother and my stepfather (we'll call him Jimmy) had a terrible fight, a screaming, lamp-breaking kind of fight. I think I remember a kitten being thrown across the room. My mother swears this isn't true. I remind her that she was too hopped up to remember anything clearly, but in my heart I know that memory is a trickster, especially the memories of children toward their parents, and it might be me who is misremembering, from my youthful perspective, from ancient resentment seeking to make things even worse than they were. In any case, I don't usually tell the part about the kitten, and the fight culminated in my mother kicking Jimmy out. Early the next morning, I heard my brother Adam shouting.

"Mom, Mom, Jimmy's crawling up the driveway!"

My room was a little rectangle that had been walled off the corner of the living room with flakeboard and a plywood veneer door, and I leapt out of bed and got to the doorway in time to see my mother stalking down the hall toward me, Adam at her back. Her blond hair was limp and ragged from sleep, her mouth bore smudged traces of the lip gloss she perennially wore, and her white satin bathrobe was open and billowing behind. Running toward me, she looked like a demented angel.

"He what?"

She crossed the shag carpet, olive green like the house, and continued past me out the front door, and Adam and I ran after. In the dim purple light of predawn, we could just make out Jimmy, wearing the grey uniform of his security guard job at the local campus of the state university, crawling on his hands and knees up the driveway toward his car. It was warm, so it must have been summer. The crickets were still spreading their low hum across the surface of the Earth. I felt the dew on the grass, and blades stuck to my bare feet. Our front yard sloped up from the street, while the driveway had been dug out and graded level with the ground, and a low stone wall edged the yard where it met the pavement. In my mind, it all happened in the blink of an eye, and in slow motion: Jimmy crawling on all fours, my mother swooping across the lawn like she was rappelling down a cliff face. Just as Jimmy was about to gain the shelter of the car, my mother launched herself off the wall, landing directly on his back. He was a big man, 6'2 and 250 pounds, while my mother was 5'5 and cocaine-skinny, but that cocaine fueled her blows with a fury my stepfather could not, or would not, match. All I remember is a drumbeat of fists, Jimmy covering his head to protect it. She battered him mercilessly.

Somebody must have called 911, because soon a police cruiser pulled up, and two cops stepped out. My mother sprung backward off Jimmy.

"All right, what's going on here?" one of the cops said.

"I want him arrested," my mother said, pointing at Jimmy.

"What happened?"

"He hit me."

The cops looked at Jimmy. He had managed to get to his feet, but he was staggering around the driveway, his uniform shirt ripped and spattered with blood, his eyeglasses hanging by one end, one lens cracked in a spiderweb pattern.

"*He* hit *you*?"

"You see how you cops are?" my mother said. "You always take the man's side." She began ranting about police bias and knowing her rights.

"Look, Kathleen," one cop said (my mother, as you often read in newspaper accounts and hear on television, was well known to the police), "if you don't calm down we're going to take you in."

That just made her angrier. "I don't give a fuck, I know my rights..."

She ranted some more until the police had had enough.

"Okay, get in the car."

At the police station, my mother continued her ranting and demanded her phone call. She used it to call her mother, my grandmother.

"Ma, I'm in jail."

"Good," my grandmother said, "that's right where you belong," and she hung up.

My mother, because she didn't want the police to know her own mother had hung up on her, kept talking. "Okay, Ma. Thanks, Ma. That's good, I'll wait here, then. Bye, Ma."

Somebody bailed her out, I suppose, because she came home. I don't remember it, but she must have. I am laughing as I write this. The part that's less funny is that I don't remember who came to watch us when my mother was taken away. I have vague memories of other incidents, one in particular in which my mother was carried from the house in a stretcher by first responders. At this time, I have a memory of older cousins coming to stay with us, and at other times my grandmother. But I have no memory of anyone turning up on the morning my mother was arrested. It is entirely possible that no one did. It is possible that the police took my mother away and assumed Jimmy would look after us, but I do not remember if he did, or anybody else. That makes me feel lonely.

In this way, my childhood is similar to my mother's drinking and drugging days. It is a patchwork of events; half-remembered stories that seem to form no overarching narrative.

There is a photo of me at Graceland. I have no memory of being there until, flipping through a ponderous photo album one day, I happen upon the photograph. I am standing in front of a gate fretted with musical notes. I am perhaps seven or eight, wearing a pink shirt and a blue windbreaker, my hair cut in a shoulder-length pageboy style. I am squinting against the sun. And then images come to me. A white room. For some reason, a tree trunk. A chapel, again all white. I look online for photos of the mansion. I see a white living room with leather chairs and a section of tree trunk, the trunk I see in my mind. It is lacquered and turns out to be a coffee table. I call my mother to see if she has any memory of this.

"When was I at Graceland?"

"You were at Graceland?" she says.

"There's a photo. Did you take me there?"

"I don't remember. I could have. Anything's possible, really."

It is difficult to understand your own story when you don't remember so much of it. I suppose it must be this way for my mother, too.

"I never could figure out," my mother says now, "how could I be so fucking crazy sometimes and then other times say, okay kids, we're going to get in the car and go have a picnic."

This is true. When I was about six, my mother herded my brother and me into the battered brown station wagon we used to go garbage picking in and drove us to Plymouth, Massachusetts. We had come to see the Rock. It was autumn, I think. Brown leaves settled against the driveway wall and along the roadside as we drove, and I remember black choppy water, where I imagined the Mayflower had docked and the pilgrims alighted onto the Rock, each one in my child's mind stepping on it like base in a game of tag before being allowed farther ashore. We spent the night in a hotel, my first time ever, though it was a motel, really, a one-story L-shaped motor court where cars pulled up in front of their rooms. It was yellow, and I remember being delighted by this. To this day, for me all the most cheerful things in the world are yellow. We ate bologna and peanut butter and jelly sandwiches, and my mother let us stay up to watch Johnny Carson.

The reason she was capable of such broad swings of mood is probably that in addition to being an alcoholic and a drug addict, my mother has what was then called manic depression. It is probably why she was an alcoholic and a drug addict, or at least part of the reason. Doctors had not yet come to grips with how to treat bipolar disorder in the 70s, not really. My mother drank and took drugs and ran riot, and people called her a wild child. Nobody questioned why she did these things. That was just Kathy. Nobody said anything when she watched a woodworking show on public television and decided she could make her own furniture. She put all our things out on the curb and called the Salvation Army to come take them away, then went to Johnson's Hardware and bought lumber, a circular saw, and other tools. The next day, she realized she had no idea how to make furniture, but by then the Salvation Army had come and taken everything away.

The chaos in my mother's mind came first. The chaos creates the desire for something to calm the storm, so the addict drinks and takes drugs, and that creates more chaos. My mother left my stepfather Jimmy at the altar. He called her that night crying.

"Katherine, why did you do that to me?" (Nobody could figure out why he always called her Katherine when her name was Kathleen).

She didn't know, she said. She had just panicked. They rescheduled the wedding for the following day. She showed up, and they were married.

Many years later, my cousin Amy was sitting in the audience at the Phil Donahue Show, and during the break they announced that they would be doing an upcoming episode on people who left somebody at the altar and asked if anyone in the audience knew somebody who fit the bill. My cousin raised her hand.

"Me, me! My Aunt Kathy did!"

So, they called my mother and asked if she'd like to be on the show. She agreed, much in the way she agreed to many things without really thinking them through, much the way she took any drug that was handed to her without knowing what it was.

"Uh...yeah, okay. Sure, I'll do that."

At five o'clock on the morning the show was to air, a limousine pulled up in front of my mother's apartment to drive her the three hours to New York City. She didn't answer her door and pretended she wasn't home. She left Phil Donahue at the altar.

When I was about seven, I went to live with my father. My father always said my mother traded me to him for the house. My mother says my father told me she would never let me see him again, and I cried so much she gave in and let him take me. When you are the child of an addict, you either misbehave to get attention, or you try to become invisible. You are very, very good. If you can be good enough, maybe they will choose you over the drug. Now, for whatever reason, my mother had given me away. We were living in the back of my father's beauty salon because he said he couldn't afford rent with all the alimony he paid my mother, and one day as I waited in my father's Datsun outside the salon, the car began rolling backward down the hill. My father hadn't set the brake, and I was rolling backward toward traffic. Instead of calling for help, I slid down in the passenger seat and closed my eyes. Just about the time I expected impact from an oncoming car, the driver's door opened and my father jumped in and pulled the emergency brake.

"Why didn't you call me?"

It had honestly never occurred to me. I didn't want to draw attention. *Be easy. Don't be any trouble. Maybe somebody will keep you.*

When the addict puts aside alcohol and drugs, they seek new ways to create chaos. When my mother got sober, she kept company with unsavory men, dashed from interest to interest, played outrageous practical jokes. You would call her and she would say things like, "Talk fast 'cause the cats are eating the phone wire."

When I was a sophomore in college, my mother used my student loan money to bail her boyfriend out of jail. On the morning of his court date, she stood outside the courthouse waiting for him, but he didn't come. When it became clear he was going to miss his court date and she would forfeit the bond, she crossed the street to a pay phone and called in a bomb threat. Because the loan was meant to pay my dorm fees for the year, I had to move out of my university apartment and spent the year sleeping in my boyfriend's room. He lived one flight down in the same dorm. You needed a resident sticker on your student ID to get into the building. These were good for one semester. I had lived there a month before being kicked out, so I had the sticker and came and went all of the first semester without any trouble. But at the beginning of the second semester, since I was not an official resident, I didn't get a sticker, so I had to rely on my boyfriend to sign me in at night. For a few weeks, he met me at the guard's desk in the lobby, I would print my name in the ledger, and he would sign next to Visiting. Sometime in the third or fourth week, I was exiting the elevator on the fifth floor when I heard somebody call my name. I turned. It was the RA, John.

"Can I see your student ID, please?"

It was over. John had seen me coming and going all semester. He was going to check my ID, confirm I was no longer a resident, and kick me out. I handed it over. He reached in his pocket and withdrew a roll of resident stickers for semester 2, smoothed one in place on my card, and handed it back.

"Okay, you're good to go."

Even now, I cry thinking of John's kindness, and my shame at needing it.

I stayed the rest of the academic year. My boyfriend's housemates had another person in the apartment, sitting on the couch, using the shower, taking up space. They didn't believe my mother had taken my student loan money. Of course they didn't. Who would? Even she convinced herself she didn't take it. She maintains I said she could have it.

None of these roommates speak to my ex-boyfriend or me anymore.

Chaos begets chaos. This is what happens. One generation's problems become the next. My mother didn't have an easy life. So she drank and took drugs, and my siblings and I didn't have easy lives because of it, nor did anyone who came in contact with us. But my mother couldn't see it because of her self-centeredness and narcissism. Drugs and alcohol have a way of making you see only your own needs. I think this is why she took them. My mother was in her own kind of pain, pain I couldn't see or understand, because of my self-centeredness. This was partly the self-centeredness of childhood and partly of the victim, the child of an alcoholic and later the 'adult child of an alcoholic.' My mother drank and took drugs to try to feed the needs that weren't being met by the people in her life, to stoke her own pain, to hold it close and pet it, just as I fixated on being the adult child of an alcoholic, to stoke my pain and hold it close.

When my mother got sober, she sometimes took me to her Alcoholics Anonymous meetings. In the beginning, this may have been because my father hadn't allowed me to see her for several years, and when we first began visiting again, we had trouble finding things to talk about. Other members brought their children, too, and we sat in the back and ate powdered doughnuts while our parents told stories of using and the chaos it had caused in their lives and the lives of their families. Each meeting ended with the recitation of the Serenity Prayer, mostly attributed to the American theologian Reinhold Niebuhr and adopted by the AA as a mantra for how to quiet the demons that lead an alcoholic to drink.

God grant me the serenity to accept the things I cannot change, the courage to change the things I can, and the wisdom to know the difference.

I heard the prayer so many times that before long I had learned it by heart, and would recite it to myself along with the adults at the front of the room. For years, I smugly offered it as advice to friends who were hung up on their own resentments, anger at parents, at lack, whatever. I thought I was better. I thought I was over it.

The trouble is, when an addict stops using, they continue to be the person they were. If they work the program, they hopefully become a better person, but the nature of the addict, at least in my experience, remains the same. My mother had as an addict and continued to have as a person in sobriety a big personality, what most addicts would recognize as the egomaniac with an inferiority complex. She held court at family picnics, striving to tell stories, to say and do outrageous things, to be the center of attention. This personality can be a marvelous thing. She retains the glorious sense of fun that makes her beloved of children and party guests. There is a photo of my brother in the bath in which my mother has covered him from head to toe in Crazy Foam. Both are laughing deliriously. When she still drove, before pulling out of the driveway, my mother would say, "Buckle your seatbelts, because remember..." and she had uttered the phrase so often that every child in the car, whether hers or not, would shout in unison, "A dead kid is a no-good kid!"

This big personality was put to noble use. She is an outspoken proponent of civil rights and a community activist. She successfully campaigned to save a nature preserve from being paved over and a highway run through it. She raised money for Christmas presents for underprivileged children. She fought a years-long battle against the use of eminent domain to seize a neighborhood full of homes to make way for a commercial and residential development.

But for me as a shy teenage girl and young adult, that outsized personality was difficult to compete with. I tried to emulate it, but it felt unnatural, like putting on my mother's clothes, just as I did her hip-huggers and platform shoes as a child. No matter what I did, I still felt like I was standing in her shadow.

71

One spring weekend when I was home from my freshman year of college, my mother and I went to a breakfast and lunch place we loved on a leafy road near her apartment. The placed was called Jack's, though the proprietor was Joe and always had been. When my sister Jennifer was young, she would walk to Jack's after school and sit at the counter drinking a soda and waiting for my mother. When my mother came in, if Jennifer asked for a slice of pie, Joe would say, "Don't give it to her, she's got candy in her pocket." It was that kind of place.

Joe hadn't seen me in almost a year, and when I walked in, he looked up from the flattop grill, wiped his hands on his apron and came to the counter. "Kathleen, your daughter is *beautiful*." Bee-yoo-tee-ful, he pronounced it.

My mother laughed nervously and fluffed her hair. "I was pretty good-looking myself in my day, you know."

"Yeah, I remember you, you were all right, but your daughter is *beautiful*."

I winced, and my mother's face fell. She had been looking for a compliment and Joe had insulted her instead. He did it, I knew, to punish her. I've just called your daughter beautiful. Can't you be proud of that? I felt so bad for her. But I was also a little pleased. Because, yes. Can't you be proud of that? Do you really need all the attention, all the time? Can't you be a little proud of me? Even as I was pleased to see her cut down a notch, I was ashamed to feel that way. I am ashamed today thinking of it. Because my mother's whole life has been a quest for validation. All the wit, all the antics, all of it has been to get attention, because underneath it all she never felt loved.

I went to a therapist. Week after week I told her my problems, my terrible childhood, our stories. She listened and asked me how it made me feel. I said it made me feel like shit, and she nodded and made notes on her notepad. After a while, I felt I wasn't getting from it what I'd heard one got from therapy—relief, perspective, peace—so I went to another therapist. I sat on a leather sofa in his tweedy office in the West Village of New York City, and told him about my childhood, all the terrible things my mother did. He nodded and looked at me, waiting for me to say something else. I'd say it, and he'd make notes, and wait. I'd say something else, and he'd write that down, too. After a few weeks, I told him I felt I wasn't getting anywhere. He said I could switch therapists if I wanted. His feelings wouldn't be hurt. So I went to a third therapist. For weeks, I told her about my childhood, the terrible things that had happened to me. Finally, one week she leaned forward in her chair and said, punctuating her points by slapping the back of her right hand in the palm of her left, "Look. That's terrible. These things happened, and they're terrible, and that's a shame, but it's done. Get over it and move on." And I paused, and I thought, Oh, is that what I'm supposed to do? All right, then, I'll move on. It was one of the best pieces of advice I've ever received, but doing it is work, and it's work that never ends.

We are all in my family, to one extent or another, addicts. For most of my family, it is alcohol or drugs, or both. For many years I told myself I was the only one who was not addicted to something. I never took drugs because I was afraid I would become addicted, and I abstained from alcohol almost completely because I simply didn't like the taste, and I felt all this made me well adjusted. I had beaten the addiction, evaded the family's Achilles heel. But I hadn't. I was addicted to being a victim. The therapist was right. You do have to move on. So I did. I stopped telling stories about my childhood and all the terrible things my mother did, and I thought I was better.

When I was twenty-five, I met a man we'll call Paul. He was seventeen years older than me, and tall. He drank every night but maintained he wasn't an alcoholic. He was loud and outgoing and the life of the party. He said he should find somebody his own age and stop wasting his time with me. Eventually he did. Then he called and asked me to take him back, so I did. Then he left me again. He called again wanting to reconcile, and again I agreed. Then he left again. This went on for years. Finally, one day when he called, I said no. I thought I had learned my lesson.

The next one, who we'll call Deacon, was taller still. He was a recovering alcoholic and told insightful stories about his drinking days and the selfishness of the alcoholic personality, and I thought, Ah hah, I have found somebody who understands his addiction and will be a better mate because of it. He had a wife with whom he claimed still to be together, but who lived 1,200 miles away, so I thought, That's okay, they're not really married; they just haven't got divorced yet. But he kept a strict limit on how often we saw each other. Saturdays and Sundays I stayed at his place. Friday nights he insisted on being alone.

"If I haven't figured out what to do with myself by next Friday night, you can start coming Friday nights, too."

Eventually I got tired of waiting for him to decide I was worth spending Friday nights with. I was taking custody of my baby sister and moving to Savannah, so that would be the end of it. He moved home, promptly divorced his wife, and began a fling with a former girlfriend from New Orleans. When she left him, he asked me to take him back, but I said no. This time I said no the first time and stuck to it. He turned up at my place in Georgia and I made him sleep on the couch. I'm better, I told myself.

The next, Noble, was remarkably tall, 6' 4, with dark brown hair and blue eyes. He drank, and I mean he *drank*. Once I caught him knocking back the dregs of his previous night's whisky at nine o'clock in the morning. He told interminable stories about his exploits in local politics and expounded the similarities between himself and Winston Churchill. He kept me on the phone until four o'clock in the morning. I had to work the next day, but I listened. Be easy. Be kept. He told me he loved me, then he told me he didn't, then he told me he didn't mean that and he did love me after all. After a while, I got tired of him taking it back, and one day when he said he didn't love me I took him at his word and left him. He called me first nightly, then weekly, then every few months, left slurred messages on my voicemail trying to get back with me. For years I never answered his calls.

Somewhere in there, I realized I hadn't escaped the addiction that plagued so many members of my family. It had just taken a different form. I was addicted to men who leave. For the child of an addict, even if your parent stops using, comes home nights, spends time, there is a thing that doesn't go away so easily. The feeling that you weren't wanted, that however smart you were, however funny, however pretty, the drug was always more alluring to your addict parent. If you can find a lover who stays, for whom you are more alluring, then you are loved. But that's the problem with this subconscious stratagem for correcting the past. It is doomed from the outset. In order for it to work, you have to choose somebody who is irresistibly drawn to some substance, then lure them away from it, to you. It didn't work with the addict parent, which is why you are trying to do it in the first place, and because the new dynamic is based on the old, it won't work now.

As if to drive home the message beyond all doubt, first Deacon and then Noble later died. Before their time, in gruesome fashion. After that, I decided to take a break from relationships for a while. I needed to sort my own issues before I could be a good partner for somebody else, or choose someone who would be a good partner to me. This is the same thing addicts are advised to do for the first two years of their recovery. God grant me the serenity to accept the things I cannot change, the courage to change the things I can, and the wisdom to know the difference. It is advice I am still learning to follow.

This is all the wisdom I can bring to this right now. Maybe later there will be more. That's how it is with a life like this. There are other repercussions for the child of an alcoholic, and I'm still working through them. You can look them up. Control freak? Check. Hypervigilant? Check. Excessive need for order? Check. I am tyrannical with a vacuum cleaner. I clean the house and then stalk its rooms for days scouting for stray dust. I spot a piece and pluck it from the floor, hold it up accusingly between thumb and forefinger and say, "What's this, lint?"

My mother is still dealing with the repercussions of being bipolar, still creating chaos, and both she and the rest of us have to deal with it. Sometimes she doesn't take her medication. Various of my mother's counselors and visiting nurses have told me that people with bipolar disorder often stop taking their medication as much as seven times before they accept that they need it to function normally. For my mother, the count surely stands at more than one hundred. We can tell when she's missed a few doses. She laughs in a way that can best be described as maniacal. Once she tried to tell my sisters and me about something funny she'd seen on television, one of those shows that airs surveillance video of people doing stupid things. What she was trying to tell us involved a guy robbing a convenience store and the owner pelting him with canned goods, candy bars, and anything else that was ready to hand. She sat in a mustard yellow velvet Barcalounger she'd scavenged from the back of the Salvation Army, near the fish tank she'd filled with plastic fish and a cerulean blue plastic diver, trying to tell the story, and laughing more and more uncontrollably.

"And then the stupid robber—and then the stupid robber, he ..."

Then she would break off laughing. In the end, she laughed so hard she couldn't finish the story. We asked her the question we always ask when she laughs like this: Did you take your medication? To this day we don't know what the stupid robber did, and we're afraid to bring it up because she'll start laughing again, that uncontrollable, maniacal laugh.

I really don't know what the point is of me telling you all this. In a way, I think it's dangerous to try to name the point. It leads to moralizing and an effort to attach meanings to other people's lives that suit your purpose, not theirs.

My mother's stories do not need to have a moral, nor does her life, nor does anyone's. These things happened. Together they make a life, a series of lives, mine and hers and those of my siblings, and everybody any of us came into contact with. Anton Chekhov wrote that there are six principles of a good story: "1. absence of lengthy verbiage of a political-social-economic nature; 2. total objectivity; 3. truthful descriptions of persons and objects; 4. extreme brevity; 5. audacity and originality; flee the stereotype; and 6. compassion." I don't know about the others, and total objectivity is impossible in memoir in any case. But I have tried mightily to uphold at least number six: compassion.

An old friend of my mother's, who called himself Bob the Mental (I think he would be genuinely pleased, if he were still alive, for me to use his real name) once gave me a piece of advice, probably the best piece of advice I've ever received: You have to take life on life's terms. And I thought, That's damn right. These are the terms. My mother drank and took drugs. For a long time, I was angry at her. And then, somehow, I wasn't. Somehow, I had learned the difference between the things I could and could not change and, in the case of my mother anyway, had accepted them. I have not found serenity yet, but hopefully that will come in time.

I do not mean to suggest that I have forgotten, or should forget, the bad memories, the things my mother did that caused me pain. That would be unfair, both to me and to her. Those things sprang from her pain as much as mine and are part of the fabric of her life. To deny them would be to deny that she has risen above them, has managed to survive. It would be to deny the sense of fun and adventure that are the most enduring qualities of hers I remember. To fixate on the bad things would also be to insist on placing myself at the center of my mother's world, which is where a child belongs, not a grown woman with sins of her own. It would be to remain someone I no longer am, a person I used to be, instead of the person I am now. I don't know for how long I will remain this person. I should pay attention to it. Hopefully I am a good person. Hopefully next time I will choose a man who doesn't leave. Hopefully I will be someone the next me won't wince to remember.

Most importantly, perhaps, it would be to deny that, somehow, despite everything, when I think of my mother, the first thing I remember is our trip to Plymouth. I wanted to stay in that hotel room, forever, with that mother. Not the mother who sank wedged between the dryer and the wall crying because she was supposed to pick me up from school but was so drunk she couldn't find the car keys, but this mother, who I can see now, sitting up in bed beneath a shiny motel quilt, with her son, blond like her, and me, her daughter, with chestnut hair and a gap where I'd lost a tooth, laughing at Johnny Carson, the blue glow of the television lighting up her blond hair and her open, laughing face.

BOYS IN MASKS

We are wearing our costumes, but we're too old to trick-or-treat. We're on our way to a party. I'm a vampire. I'm wearing one of my father's barber capes backwards and I've dabbed the corner of my mouth with my grandmother's old Avon lipstick to look like dripping blood. Andy is a devil in red plastic horns from Woolworth's. Benj is in a top hat and tails he borrowed from his grandfather, who drives a limousine, and when we ask him what he is, he says he's the ghost of Teddy Roosevelt.

Walking past the Revolutionary War monument at the fort, we have to watch the sidewalk to see our own feet. It's five o'clock and already dark. There's almost no moon, and the night is blue sapphire, tufts of cloud streaked here and there like giant hands have stretched cotton candy across the sky. During the war, a Continental soldier was always stationed at the top of the stone obelisk to watch the river approach from the Sound. If all was clear, he hung one lantern. If he spotted the British approaching, he was to hang two. We look up. One light burns in the square window at the tower's peak. The British are not coming tonight.

Andy and Benj are tall for their age, and I like walking between them. The girls are a head taller than most of the boys, and I like that Andy and Benj tower over me, tall and reedy and clattering about as I do. The whole group has always been eight, four boys and four girls, but lately it's been more Benj and Andy and me. Especially Benj. The cool air settles like dry ice on my face and the wispy crystalline hairs of my arms, transparent as moth's wings. My breasts, so lately like lumps of melting sugar, have begun to round and plump, and I like standing with my hands on my waist, acting as though I'm challenging but secretly enjoying the feel of the curve inward

85

and then the sloping out into hips. We prance and leap and shudder at each other's closeness. The air between us vibrates.

We pass the mechanic's where my grandmother always took her car. She went nowhere else because the place was owned by a man called Craig, who was half Native American, and she said they were honest people because they'd been robbed by the settlers and knew how it felt to be swindled. And here's the Dew Drop Inn, and we stop and lean on the wall outside and listen to the tinkling glass and chatter within. Lights above the bar like pure fire and the men's faces red from laughter and drink and the place is blazing like Hell. Here's Mr. Simmons, old fisherman's cap worn with a rakish tilt and a chest like a barrel you'd ride over Niagara Falls, and he's telling how Clarence, the town's only homeless man, came to live rough. An old argument, and everybody has their opinion, but Mr. Simmons is taken seriously because as a merchant marine in 1932 he heard Hitler speak and wrote home that he was a loony-bird. We move on and the laughter and clinking glass float away behind us like burnt ash.

Outside the liquor store, Benj and Andy stop just shy and lean against the cold, white brick. I look older and am always sent in to buy. Inside, I stroll down the aisle like I belong there. I take a pack of wine coolers from the refrigerator case and carry it to the counter. Mr. Watrous of the mongoose moustache and crying eyes is working so his wife can answer the door for trick-or-treaters.

"I don't know what happened, I turned around and mine were all grown up, now they're having kids of their own. Youth is over in a heartbeat, young lady. Enjoy it while it lasts."

Andy puts the wine coolers in his backpack so we don't get stopped. We cross the road on the way back, past the park where we used to go sledding and then our old elementary school. I think of the day the gymnasium roof caved in under heavy snow and we all sat in the playground in our coats waiting for our parents to pick us up. No one is more nostalgic than a child.

We pass the Avery land, where years before they dug a hole and buried the old stone house, plowed it right in whole, and where before that the barn had burned in the middle of the night. Neighbors knocked on doors, and we all came out and watched the orange glow just beyond the tree line. The ghost did it, people said, the pretty blond girl shot through the eye by a boy because she wouldn't do it. It's haunted still. I look down, counting cracks in the sidewalk and humming to myself.

Benj's hand brushes mine as we walk, and we both pull away. I blush, and Benj jumps and grabs onto a tree limb to distract attention, swinging from one arm like a monkey, then drops and takes a flying leap onto Andy's back.

"Giddyap, boy," Benj says. "Heidi's waiting."

Benj pinches Andy's cheek, and he shoulders him off and grins.

"Andy loooooooves Heidi," Benj says. "He wants to have her baaaaaaabies."

"Somebody needs an anatomy lesson," I say, and they both laugh.

On the far edge of the elementary school, we pause at the path that cuts through the woods. We used to use it as a shortcut home from school, but older kids use it as a party spot at night—sometimes you find beer bottles and condoms—so we continue along the road.

What moon there was is somewhere behind the bottle-blue night and the wind has lifted and the trees are quivering. As we walk, I think I hear something. I turn to look, and three boys in masks are walking behind us. Werewolf masks. They're older than us, taller and bulkier, in long, dark coats and combat boots, and the masks are grey with white teeth bared in a growl. I can tell they're boys by the way they move. They're about ten feet behind us. I turn around. Benj and Andy turn to see what I'm looking at, then they turn back, too.

We walk quietly for a minute. I turn back and they're still there.

"Hey," I say casually.

They don't say anything. They just watch us. I turn away again. We walk on a little way, and we hear them still behind us.

Andy turns around and walks backward. "You guys going to a party? Trick or treating?"

They don't answer. Andy turns back to us. "So, anyway," he says, like we're returning to a conversation we were having, but nobody talks.

At my development, we turn in. As we round the bend, I look out of the corner of my eye and see their silhouettes. My head starts to buzz, and my arms and legs tingle. After a while the feeling slows my stride, and as though my legs won't work, I stop, and Benj and Andy stop with me. We all turn, and the boys in masks have stopped, too. They're just standing there. They don't say anything, just stare at us. They look from one of us to another, turning their heads in stiff, unnatural pivots. We turn again and continue on, and they're still behind us.

We walk, they walk.

We stop, they stop.

Benj stops and turns.

"Okay, guys, ha ha, scare the younger kids. But it's over now. We've got a girl with us, it's not funny anymore."

The boys in masks just stare. As if by some secret signal, they turn their heads in unison from Benj to me. I can see their eyes behind the masks.

"Knock it off," Andy says.

They just stare.

"You're scaring her," Benj says.

The boys don't move or speak. Benj turns, watching them over his shoulder, and we start walking again. A little farther on, we stop again and turn. The boys in masks are just standing there again, but closer now, about six feet away. We turn and walk, and then something breaks in us and we burst into a run. I turn to look and they're running after us. Benj and Andy grab my elbows and we run on. We're in my neighborhood, so I lead, darting in and out between buildings. We duck through into a back yard then down a driveway across a street. We hear feet pounding hard on pavement and know they're behind us. We're lighter, more fleet, but the boys in masks run hard. My building is close and we're pushing for it, pushing. At the building behind mine, I feign a run at one of the apartment doors but at the last minute veer for the side yard. Benj and Andy follow and we crack-the-whip round the side of the building and toward my apartment's back door.

I vault the steps and pray it's open and it is and we rush in and as I turn to close the door behind me, I see the boys in masks running at me. I shoot the bolt and run to the front door to make sure it's locked. Benj and Andy are in a jumble behind me and when we're sure it's locked, too, we bend double, catching our breath. I edge up to the wall by the window and look out. The boys in masks are standing stock still in the yard, staring at me. I pull the cord and close the drapes.

We sit side by side on the couch. Andy sets the wine coolers on the coffee table. The party should be starting now. It's about a half-mile down the road, but the boys in masks may still be out there. Benj goes and kneels on the floor before my videos. He pulls one out and holds it up so we can see the case. We nod, and he pops it into the player. We've seen it at least ten times, but we lean back and watch.

Awhile later we look out, and the boys in masks are gone. But we're not going anywhere tonight. We return to the sofa and finish the movie. I'm only half watching. I'm thinking about the boys in masks, and I don't understand why people have to ruin things. I look over at Benj and Andy, and think, *They'll never be like that.*

The above is a story I wrote about something that really happened. But the truth is much different. I had no friends with me, in particular no boy friends who could perhaps make me feel a bit safer; I was alone. I was not in my Halloween costume; I was not coming home from buying wine coolers. I was walking home from school, and the boys picked up my trail right where the nicer neighborhood began to give way to the projects in which I lived, not a subdivision or a neighborhood, with all their connotations of middle class.

I don't know why I changed those details. Maybe I wasn't ready to confront the fact that I was alone, a twelve-year-old girl, being followed by six older boys in wolf masks. Maybe the metaphor felt too real. Maybe I wanted to make myself feel more mature by buying alcohol. Maybe the fact that the boys started trailing me as we approached the projects hit too close to home. Maybe it said something about the new danger that had entered my life when we moved into those projects. Maybe it said that, since they had picked up my trail in the regular neighborhoods outside the projects, I was seen as inferior, a person of no value who could be preyed upon without consequence.

Some of it was true. I did pass the site of the Avery house. The barn behind the house had burned down when I was nine or ten, and there had been talk of a girl killed there because she would not have sex with her boyfriend. Perhaps that also felt too close to me, in the real incident a twelve-year-old girl already being circled by boys, and sometimes men. The house had indeed been pushed into a hole in the ground, or at least I think it did. That is my memory of what happened, but memory is unreliable and often fills in holes or changes facts to suit our own narrative of ourselves, so that is possible.

They put up a nursing home on the land where it had stood. My grandmother had lived in that nursing home. Perhaps I did not want to think about her there, a plastic butter tub full of pills on her kitchen table. Perhaps I did not want to think about her approaching death, and how, when it did come, when I was 20 years old, I said to myself, though my mother and father were still alive, *now I am all alone.*

That constant internal editing is part of the shame of poverty: what we permit people to know, what we will not admit even to ourselves, those things which are so shameful that we write them out of our own internal construction of ourselves. You don't even always know that you're doing it. You do it to survive the shame.

I began to notice myself about the same time men did— *because* men did, in fact. I had just turned twelve and they had begun to look. I had been a fat girl, then one day, when I was about eleven or so, I stopped eating for no particular reason and grew five or six inches. I noticed looking in the mirror one night that I was thin. I took off my shirt and stared, fascinated, at my waist, the way it curved inward then out into hips.

Everywhere I went, boys and men began to catcall me.

"Hey, girl."

"Hey, wait up."

"Yo, hold up, let me talk to you a sec."

"Hola, mami."

"Tú eres muy bonita."

Kissing sounds.

At first it was flattering that boys were noticing the little fat girl I still was in my mind. Then it became intrusive. Eventually it became frightening.

One day my father took me to Railroad Salvage to buy a new mattress. I was wearing short shorts, white, my little girl self not thinking anything except that it was hot out. We stepped onto the sidewalk, and a man leaning against the wall outside the store stared at me. I remember thinking he was old—he was probably only 45 or so—but I flushed, proud that he'd noticed me and yet knowing he was a grown man and shouldn't be looking at a girl my age. My father glared at him and grabbed me by the elbow and swept me past him into the store.

Another time a friend and I were sitting on my front steps in the projects and a boy came over.

"Yo, yo, what you ladies up to today?"

My father burst through the screen door and yelled at the boy to get the hell out of here before he called the cops, and the poor boy ran off. I didn't know the boy, but he didn't seem to present any menace. He was just trying to make time, as all boys were.

But some people did present menace. A lot of it.

One day as I was walking home from visiting my grandmother, I noticed a blue Toyota driving very slowly behind me. I remember it was summer because the leaves had begun to turn from soft green to a deeper forest green color. I had learned from living in the projects that you had to be alert to anything that didn't look or feel right, so I stopped and leaned against the fence at the edge of my grandmother's senior home, hoping the car would pass. But it didn't.

The driver pulled over to the side of the road and pretended to look at a map. He looked young, with black hair and glasses, but that was all I could see, looking out of the corner of my eye. I pushed away from the fence and kept walking, then turned to look over my shoulder. The car was moving again, going very slowly, keeping behind me. This was all the proof I needed. I had reached the border of Colonial Manor, where I had lived before we moved to the projects, and I knew its secret places and back ways, so I ran and quickly slipped between two buildings facing the street. I knew that there was a grassy area behind them, then two buildings opposite and beyond those a cul-de-sac. But most importantly, there was no road in where I had run. The driver would have to continue on for another hundred feet or so before he could take the first left turn into the development.

I moved to the edge of the second two buildings and hid behind the building on the right so I could see both the entrance road and the cul-de-sac. There was a dumpster just behind the building, so he wouldn't be able to see me from the main road, and I was able to peek out just enough to see the cul-de-sac in the gap between the building and the drainpipe without being seen. I watched and waited. A few minutes later, the blue Toyota appeared in the cul-de-sac. He drove around it in a circle, stopped for a minute, as though the driver was trying to figure out which direction I had taken, then moved off again.

I crept forward to the front edge of the building and peeked around. No Toyota. Using the parked cars for cover, I moved around the perimeter of the cul-de-sac, watching for the car. The way was clear, so I raced across to the road and ducked between the buildings facing the road and the buildings behind it that faced the road in the middle of the development. There was a long stretch of cover there, so I moved from building to building, watching for the Toyota. When I saw it moving past my location towards the intersection behind me, I took off running to the end of that stretch and peeked out.

The Toyota was coming back down that main road, so I ducked behind the building and crouched, and watched it pass my location and drive down the hill. Once it was out of sight, I tore across the road, past one of two buildings we had lived in in that development and reached a woody dirt path that connected Colonial Manor and the projects where I lived. And I waited. I had a good view of the hilltop and the main road from here, and a minute later the Toyota crested the hill and continued straight along the main road, away from me. I turned and tore along the path and emerged in the projects and ran, weaving between a wide swath of buildings in the center of the projects, which made it inaccessible by car, until I made it home, where I ran in and locked the door.

It was probably just some random creeper, but a couple of years later, I was watching the news (I was a weird kid), and they reported that a serial killer had been arrested for the murders of eight women in Connecticut, one in the next town over from me. They flashed his mug shot on the screen, and then showed a photo of his car. It was a blue Toyota. I have no idea if it was Michael Ross who followed me that day or not, but in the mug shot, he had black hair and was wearing glasses. Either way, whoever it was, they were trolling this area because it was not a good neighborhood and likely an easier place in which to find a girl he might lure into his car.

When I walked the halls in school, boys watched me pass. Not just the poor boys; the rich boys, too. But I was shy and so were they, even though they were rich. Some of us had been children together, and we were trying to work out these new things we were thinking and feeling about each other. We knew about sex. Later, in college, a friend of mine told me that she and her sister had a sex box; they cut up magazine photos of men in their underwear and put them in the box. They didn't know exactly what sex was, but they knew it had something to do with men and underwear. When I was twelve, the sex box was in our heads. We looked and smiled and mentally put each other in the box. It also made me feel like I had value, when for most of the rest of the time I didn't.

Look at me, I thought.

As I have said, most of the boys, like me, were shy. One boy, though, was bolder than the rest. Luis was 14 years old and a ninth grader and, like me, lived in the projects. In a few months he would graduate and move up to high school. He had a brush of wispy hair on his upper lip and his hair cut like one of the older boys. I knew him in passing, but not much more than that. He would smile and say hello as I was leaving school, and sometimes I would notice him sitting on the hill and watching as I ran the outdoor track during recess.

One day he approached me in the hall as I was walking from one class to the next. I was wearing my mother's hand-me-down hip huggers with a wide white belt and a T-shirt with a sparkly unicorn on it.

"Hey," he said.

"Hey," I said.

We talked for a few minutes in the way that adolescents do, and then he asked me out. I was only thirteen and not ready to date, but I was babysitting that night and told him he could come keep me company if he wanted to.

Maybe we will hold hands, I thought. *Maybe he will kiss me.*

He readily agreed, and I gave him the address and we said we'd see each other that night.

I was babysitting for a grandmother who had custody of her son's two children and worked the night shift at a local ice cream shop and eatery. I sat for her often.

Luis arrived at eight, as we'd arranged. The children were still very young—one a toddler and the other about six months old—so they had gone to bed at seven-thirty. I had the TV on, so we sat down on the couch and watched TV and talked a little bit. Pretty soon Luis reached out and took my hand, and I let him hold it. Then he leaned in for a kiss, and I let him kiss me. Just a peck. Then he leaned in again and began to kiss me for real this time. I was not ready for that. He pushed me down on my back on the sofa. I told him to get off me and he wouldn't and began reaching for his zipper, so I reached down and grabbed his nuts and squeezed them as hard as I could. Maybe it's because I took karate lessons briefly at a young age and have always worked out, but I have always been, as my sister Charity has said, 'freakishly strong.' He screamed and pushed and pulled at my hands and finally broke my grip, and he curled up in pain and I rolled out from beneath him. Go for the nuts, my brother always told me, and if you can't reach them, go for the eyes. Put your thumbs on the eyes and push in as hard as you can. They'll pop right out.

"Get out," I yelled.

But he lay in the fetal position on the couch clutching his crotch.

"Get out," I repeated, and I grabbed him by the hair and pulled him off the sofa and he hit the floor. He called me a fucking bitch then and reached for my leg and I stomped on his hand, and when he rolled away I kicked him in the ribs. Then it was fairly easy to drag him across the floor, open the back door, haul him up by his shirt collar and the back of his jeans, and shove him out. I closed the door and locked it, and then made sure the windows were locked, then ran to the front of the apartment and did the same.

I paced back and forth across the living room, crying in intermittent bursts. Then Luis knocked on the back door.

"Let me in."

"Fuck off," I yelled.

Then he began banging on the window.

"Open the fucking door, you fucking bitch."

I don't know why I didn't call 911. I just...didn't. Maybe I thought they wouldn't get there fast enough. Maybe I thought it wouldn't do any good, that they would come and Luis would shrink into the shadows, the cops would take my statement and the moment they left, Luis would be at the door again.

I ran to the kitchen and grabbed the biggest knife I could find. It was a carving knife, the kind Michael Myers used. In truth, what you want if you really intend to stab somebody is something small, something less unwieldy, something they can't easily get a hold of and with which you can jab fast and repeatedly. But I only learned this later when I told my brother what had happened. As it was, I grabbed the carving knife and ran back to the window and pulled back the drapes. Luis saw the knife and stopped banging.

"If you come in this house, I will stick this thing right into your guts," I said, "and then when you're on the ground I will cut your throat."
This is how you survive in the projects. You get aggressive, and fast. If they take it to five, you go straight to eleven. Make them believe that you will kill them and not give two shits about

it. You don't have to mean it, you just have to make them think you mean it. When white people see black people talking like that and thumping their chests and holding their arms out, saying "What you gonna do, motherfucker?" and clutch their pearls and talk about 'the violence in the black community,' that's what those black men and boys are doing (and women and girls, too). They're scared and they're just trying to keep themselves alive. Like Trayvon Martin. They're just trying to get home with their bag of Skittles in one piece.

Luis backed away from the window and I let the curtains fall. I went to the couch and sat shaking and clutching the knife until the woman I was babysitting for came home. When I heard her car outside, I ran to the kitchen and returned the knife to the knife block, and when she asked me how it had gone, I said, "Fine." She was a nice lady, and I didn't want her to think I was the kind of girl who had any truck with a boy like that. Because I knew Luis would not have done that to one of the more well-off girls in school. He would not have dared. They were above his station, and I was at it.

The following morning at school, as I opened my locker, I heard snickering, and I turned around and saw some of the other kids looking at me and smirking and whispering to each other. A friend of mine at the next locker leaned in.

"That boy Luis told everybody you slept with him last night."

"What?"

"That's what he said. You didn't, did you?"

"No!"

"That's what I thought. I told my sister, no way would she sleep with him."

She and her sister, her twin, were both in Group 1 with me, and luckily all my friends in the group believed me. I don't know if it was because they simply knew I didn't want to have sex yet or because Luis was Latino and they had the racist thought 'no way would she sleep with a Puerto Rican boy,' but at that point I didn't care. I was just glad to be believed. These kids, most of them well off, believed me. They took my side. They formed a circle around me and shielded me from the thing that at that moment was making me feel like poor white trash.

I never saw Luis in school much after that, and when I did see him, I glared and he turned away, embarrassment etched on his face. And always when this happened, his friends began whispering to him urgently. I couldn't hear what they were saying, but I hoped they were asking him, "Why she so mad at you? You weren't any good? Or it ain't happen at all, you fuckin liar?"

Boys still looked at me after that, and I still felt a frisson of excitement that I was being noticed, but now my reaction was different.

Don't look at me.

It took years to overcome it. I didn't really date in high school because of it. One boy asked me to the prom and promptly shoved his tongue down my throat. I said no and brooked no offers after that.

It was not until college that I began to seriously date. When I got there, I knew immediately that I was among people who had not grown up in the projects. One thing that made that clear was the tony status of the school. It was a school where rich people went. And many of them *were* rich. But still I walked the streets, arms at the ready, fists clenched, and when a classmate asked me out, a nice boy, I knew I was safe with him and I said yes, and we stayed together all through college and a bit beyond.

But the knowledge of my vulnerability stayed with me.

Even today, when shopping for clothes, if I see a particularly girly dress or blouse, my first instinct is to say no. Don't be girly. It attracts attention. But I have reached the point where I can overcome that instinct. Because I love girly clothes, and in the circles I move in now, I don't feel like a prey animal.

But even now, in public, on the streets, I walk, fists clenched, arms at the ready. Ready for Luis, or someone like him, someone who will recognize me as poor white trash and deserving of assault. I know this is ridiculous. Middle-class and rich women get assaulted all the time. But in my head, part of me is still that thirteen-year-old girl, thinking she was chosen because she had no value and nobody would care if she was hurt.

So I clench my fists, and I walk.

BRIDGE 1

When I was 16, my father kicked me out of the house. He had nearly kicked me out when I was thirteen and he found out I was friends with a Latino boy. "I can't believe I raised a n***** lover," he said.

This time he really did kick me out. I don't remember why. I remember him throwing a videotape case across the room because I borrowed a movie with his membership and returned it a day late, and I remember calling him a piece of shit, but that may not have been the reason. It could have been anything, really. My father was a man-child with a volcanic temper and no understanding of his responsibilities as a parent.

I got a job at a pizza place in a nearby shopping plaza and moved into an apartment with two friends. The owner was a Greek immigrant. Stay in school, he said. I assured him I would. I went to school until 2:30 in the afternoon and worked at the pizza place every day until closing and then I bicycled home. If I had time, I did my homework. I couldn't keep up in math. I never could, but in junior high school, they had given me extra help. Now, my geometry teacher told me I was lazy. I was smart, she said, so I simply wasn't doing the work. When I continued to fail in math, the school moved me to a lower group in all my subjects. The math was easier, but I was bored with everything else. I was also nervous. I began blinking my eyes rapidly, compulsively, at random times. "We call this a tic," the school counselor said. I was tired. I still couldn't sleep at night, and often I was still willing myself to drift off when my alarm rang at 6:30 in the morning. So, at some point after I turned 16, I don't remember when precisely, I dropped out.

It was a relief, if I'm honest. I signed the paper withdrawing myself from school and walked down the long hall through the dimly lit foyer and out into the sunlight, and I felt free. This was not an admission of defeat for me. I still planned to go to college. This was a jettisoning of the burden of work and school and classes I hated, and it freed me up to work full time. I got a job as a properties coordinator for a musical theater company. When my class graduated, I took the GED as planned. I had intended to spend the winter studying, but when I looked at the first practice test and saw the question, 'What comes first, thunder or lightning?' I saw that there was no need. They didn't intend the test to help us in any way. It was just a piece of paper to show that they had made provision for those of us who couldn't manage high school. I took the test, and once I received my letter proving I had a high school diploma, I began looking at colleges. As I mentioned earlier, I only had enough money to make application at one school, so I spent a lot of time deciding which one to try for. I had no particular idea about getting a good job. Nobody in my family had a job at all, so I just planned on getting whatever job I could get with a humanities degree. I just wanted to write and to be in New York City. I had been there a few times. I went twice with my aunt and my cousin, first to see *Starlight Express* and then *Les Miserables*. Aunt Barbara had married a man who worked at Electric Boat and lived in a modest but nice house in a little former fishing village near us called Noank, and she tried to expose me to the world beyond the projects, for which I will forever be grateful to her. I went again when I was sixteen with a colleague at the musical theater company to pick up costumes, and again to collect the costume designer for one of the shows. New York was everything Groton was not. It was exciting and interesting and stimulating, with eight million people to talk to, all kinds of people, instead of Groton's

38,000, and it seemed to me a place where you could become somebody new.

So, I decided to apply to New York University.

"Why not go to the community college?" my mother asked when I told her. Which is to say, That is not for us. That is not for you. The local school is for you and it is as high as you should aim, which is to say, it is as high as they will let you go. They might let me go a little higher, but I would have to leave myself behind, and the things I knew of how the world treated people like me.

When I was accepted, I received a fat package full of financial aid applications. I filled them all out, and I got all the federal aid I was eligible for, but since I was essentially emancipated, in fact if not in law, NYU instructed me to apply for the loan for independent postgraduate students as well as the loan for dependent undergraduates. The undergraduate loan was need-based, but the postgraduate loan required a credit check, and I doubted I would pass it. At 19, my credit was already terrible since my father had had my car repossessed and my mother had used my social security number to get cable and then not paid the bill.

To my surprise, I got the postgraduate student loan. All that money went to NYU, though. I still needed money to get to New York and ship my things, and of course I would need to get a job once I got there to support myself. All the money I had been making working at home had gone for rent and other living expenses, so I sold my collection of Archie comics to the used bookstore in town, but it wasn't enough. I sold my typewriter, which I had bought with my first paycheck from the musical theater company. When it came time to leave, and I still didn't have enough, I sold my bicycle.

My boyfriend offered to drive me to the station the morning of my departure, and though it was twenty minutes in the opposite direction, I had booked my ticket out of Mystic, the wealthy community to the east, rather than from New London, which would have shortened the journey by nearly a half hour. He picked me up before daylight, and we drove the back roads through the purple pre-dawn. The person I wanted to see more than anyone was my grandmother, but she was ailing, and it was very early, so I asked him to drive to Noank. My aunt rose early, usually before five, so I knew I would probably find her having coffee on her porch, and I wanted to see someone familiar, someone from my family.

Something had changed. I was leaving my old life behind and heading to a future I did not know and therefore feared, and I wanted to preserve my childhood a few moments longer. But I also wanted to transform that childhood; turn it into the gentler, middle-class one I had wanted. We pulled up in front of the house and climbed the steps and sat with my aunt until it was nearly time for my train. She hugged me and wished me well, and I left.

In New York, I was surrounded by writers. They poked at my prose, challenged my ideas, taught me to interrogate them. I wrote terrible plays, and then I wrote a halfway decent one. I saw a leaflet that said, 'Tonight, Gregory Corso will read...whatever he damn well pleases,' and I thrilled at the notion that this storied poet would come and read to us, and that his writing mattered so much, that *writing* mattered so much, that nobody even cared what he read, just so long as he read.

I also had my ideas challenged in every way imaginable. I took world religion and art history and philosophy and British and American fiction. The great scholar of religion James Carse gave me a C on my paper on *I and Thou*. He said it would have been better if I had read the book. I *had*. His book *Finite and Infinite Games* became a cult hit in Silicon Valley. In English, I hated *Sister Carrie* so much I turned up to class without having finished it. Instead of scolding me, the professor made me a deal that if I could write a convincing essay on why it was a bad book, I didn't have to finish it. I wrote the essay, and thank God, I didn't have to finish the book. I still haven't read it. I keep thinking I will, but then I think the lesson I learned *because* of the book is more important than what I learned *from* it. What I learned is that it doesn't matter how you get there, the point is to grow, and there existed people in the world like my professor, who wanted you to learn and to grow and didn't care how you went about it. The learning was what mattered.

Just over a month after I started college, in the late afternoon of October 19, 1987, I was eating an early dinner with friends in our dorm's cafeteria. Trading on the New York Stock Exchange had been in freefall since it opened that day, and by the time my friends and I sat down to dinner, it had plummeted. By the time trading ended, the Dow had lost 508 points. The stock market had crashed. I knew this was important, and deeply serious, but it didn't affect my life as a college student, at least not in ways I was aware of at the time. We were making Halloween plans. It was our first one in New York City. Halloween in Greenwich Village. The Halloween parade. We were giddy. What I didn't know is that Black Monday, as it was soon called, and the period that followed, would prove to be another downward turn of the screw for American workers, and for me.

Still, I went to class, I went to work. I worked throughout my time at university; part time the first year and full time after that. Friends and dorm mates made weekly trips to the pigeon holes in the lobby to collect envelopes containing checks from parents. No such money would be coming to me from home. If you asked me where home was then, I would have said: My home is here. It's where my friends are, it's where my studies are. It's where any good thing I could expect would come from, from the work I did myself and from what I could wrest into being. So I worked. I almost didn't finish my degree in four years because I worked so much. Sometime during my sophomore year, I took a job as a proofreader in midtown, and I shuttled back and forth all day between work and classes in Greenwich Village. At the end of year three, when my advisor was helping me plan my class schedule for my final year, he told me I would have to take six classes both semesters to graduate on time. We were sitting in the library, and I stared at my credit list and the schedule in front of me, knowing that I still had to work full time while taking those classes and trying to find some way to make the numbers add up. But I couldn't, and quietly I began to cry. I didn't even have the energy to hide it.

Stuart, my advisor, had been standing at the window looking at the weather, and he noticed the silence and turned my way. When he saw me, he came to my side, gave me a quick hug and shook my shoulders. *You can do this*, the shake said. That hug and that shake got me through. Without them, I might not have made it. So many things are like that. A tiny gesture someone makes and thinks no more of, and yet thirty years later you still think about it. He never knew what he did for me that day; I never told him. I was too embarrassed, I guess. He died of prostate cancer when I was 25. I still have the last thing he wrote, a book, sitting on my shelf. I haven't read it. I have read everything else he ever wrote, but not this book. Because he died before I was able to buy it, and it feels as though once I read this book, I will have nothing left of him that is new and he will be lost to me forever. I look at the book sometimes and I think of Stuart, and I wish so badly that I had told him how he saved me.

I graduated on a Friday in May. Graduations were normally held in Washington Square Park, but for some reason, on this day they lined us up outside the sports center. Maybe they were expecting rain. If they were, it never came. It was 90 degrees by 11am, and our black robes pressed on our shoulders and backs until we were swimming in our own sweat. At noon, they marched us into the gymnasium. They had tried to decorate it with a sense of occasion, but it felt temporary, as though they were moving our class out so they could move another one in. Bill Cosby was our commencement speaker. He made us laugh. We loved him. (That's another thing we've lost).

"We are the real-world people," he said of himself and the other dignitaries on the stage. "And we don't care about you." We laughed, and he mocked our laughter. "Yeah, ha ha ha. We really don't."

Turns out he was right, but we were not ready for that particular truth just yet.

When the ceremony was over, my boyfriend and I went to lunch with our families, and then we all went to our apartment in Brooklyn. I think I had baked a cake. Friends packed up and left New York, some for home and some for holidays away. Many hadn't started job hunting yet. The following Monday, with rent to pay, I started my new job. It paid $19,000 a year.

I was lucky to get a job at all. I had graduated into a recession. Like the stock market crash, the recession was not the result of some calamity like a war. It was a paper recession. The economy had been weakening since 1989, the result, say people who know about such things, of a restrictive monetary policy from the Fed. They were trying to reduce inflation. In doing so, they also reduced economic growth. The 1986 Tax Reform Act probably contributed as well. It ended the real estate boom, which lowered property values. Real estate investments became less attractive, and jobs were lost. Then came the 1990 oil price shock, which damaged consumer and business confidence, and just like that, we were in recession. Try to explain it and it melts into thin air. By the time I graduated, the economy had recovered, but unemployment continued to rise. The country lost 1.5 million jobs in just a year. A jobless recovery, they call it. Economic growth returns; jobs do not.

The month before we graduated, *The New York Times* ran a special report about it.[2] We faced the bleakest job market in a decade or more, they told us. The number of entry-level jobs was down 30 percent. Graduating seniors put in hundreds of

---

[2] Scramble for Jobs: Graduating Into a Recession. The New York Times, April 22, 1991
https://www.nytimes.com/1991/04/22/nyregion/scramble-for-jobs-graduating-into-recession-special-report-degrees-stacks.html

applications but found nothing. My boyfriend was one of them. After several months of putting in applications and hearing nothing, he found temporary work as a messenger, but it rankled. We were told to go to college. We were told it was the path to good jobs. Now we had tens of thousands of dollars in student loan debt and were each making less than twenty thousand dollars a year, both of us in jobs we hated.

Meanwhile, I was having as much trouble sleeping as ever. The TV helped a little. My boyfriend couldn't sleep with it on, I couldn't sleep with it off. I lay awake, watching the clock: three, four, five am. Watching moonlight and shadow roll across the ceiling until dawn hit the floorboards. I dragged myself into work, every day the permanent circles under my eyes turning a deeper and deeper blue like two bruises. "Don't stay up so late partying," my boss said. I don't think I was on time for work one day in six months. In November I was fired.

We gave up our apartment in Brooklyn and moved in with my mother in Connecticut because we didn't know what else to do. Eventually, we both found work, and so did most of the unemployed.

But something had changed. You didn't notice it right away— we had a young, energetic new president and people rallied to his promises of a place called hope—but you noticed it over time. Something felt different about the world. Something felt different about America. We were less joyous, less buoyant. More fretful, more subdued. And angrier with each other.

Six months after I graduated, my student loan payments were due to begin. I arrived home from work in the early evening and found a large envelope in the mail containing a coupon book and a letter indicating my repayment amount. My monthly payment? $695. I laughed out loud. My take-home pay was about $1,300 a month. My rent was $650. Even if I didn't eat, didn't pay the light bill or the phone bill or buy subway tokens to get to and from work, I still didn't have enough to make that payment. I called my loan administrator, Sallie Mae, and explained all that, and asked if I could make a reduced payment that took my income into account. No. Not 'I'll talk to my supervisor and get back to you,' not 'how much can you afford?' Just no.

The only option I had was a hardship deferment. Well, how do I get that? I asked. The woman on the phone informed me that I would have to fill out an application and said she would send me the paperwork immediately. I waited two weeks, and when the paperwork hadn't arrived, I called them back. Your monthly payment is $695, the woman said, and you're in arrears. Yes, I said. I told the last person I spoke with that I couldn't afford that payment and she said she would send me hardship deferment paperwork. I don't have any record of that, the woman said, but I can send that paperwork out to you. Great, I said. And so began a game with Sallie Mae. They would tell me I had to pay $695 a month, I would tell them I made $1,300 a month and that $650 of that went to rent so even if I gave them every single dime I had left over I still didn't have enough to make that payment, and they would promise to send me deferment paperwork, which they would never send. Then they would call saying I was in arrears and in danger of going into default, and the whole thing would start all over again. After a few months of this, my student loans went into default.

I tried not to think about my student loans and braced for the day that they would garnish my wages. If I can get a job with a higher salary and save up a bit, I thought, maybe I can get my loans out of default and afford the payments.

As time went on and I started making a bit more money I thought, 'maybe I can start saving a bit and get my loans out of default.' But I had another obligation to meet first. My mother had had another baby, just before I left for college—my baby sister Charity—and I was spending a good deal of my income to help support her. My mother hadn't worked for years. She subsisted on welfare and food stamps. Once a month, from the time I went off to college, I went home to visit, filled the house with healthy food and bought Charity toys. As she got older, I bought her school clothes. My brother was older than me, and I was only five when my sister Jennifer was born, so there was no chance of helping them avoid the poverty of our parents. But I was an adult now, and I was determined to reach down and pull Charity out. When she was 14, I obtained legal custody of her with my mother's consent, and we moved to Savannah.

It was all worth it. Charity is the one who will break the cycle of poverty in our family. She is studying for a Master's in Social Work at Columbia University, has a job she loves, and owns a house. Her daughters, my wonderful nieces, are in a good school district, and they have nice friends. They don't have everything, but they have enough, and they have a yard to play in that looks out on a wood. Lily stalks among the trees to the creek, looking for interestingly colored rocks and imagining the things twelve-year-olds imagine, and Grace runs out in her bare feet in the morning to eat raspberries off the bushes at the tree line. And they hear no police sirens. At some time in the distant future, Charity will be able to leave that house to Lily and Grace, and they will be able to use it to buy houses of their

117

own. So I do not regret a thing. But without a bolt from the blue, I will never financially recover from my past. This is how poor people stay poor.

MY FATHER DIED
TODAY

My father was a miserable man. He died today. Good.

I wrote that sentence in my journal years ago. My father was still alive at the time, but I kept that sentence ready. I couldn't wait for it to be true. To tell you why, I have to tell you a lot of other things first.

One night when I was five or six, I heard drawers opening and closing in the kitchen, and the clang of metal. My room was a sort of add-on that had been carved out of the living room, flakeboard partitions tacked onto the paper-thin wall that abutted the kitchen, so I could easily hear what went on in there. I went in and found my mother, in her white satin dressing gown, bottle-blonde hair wild, dumping all the knives from the drawer onto a towel on the floor.

"What are you doing?" I said.

"If I don't get rid of these knives, I'm going to kill your father."

It's possible that she was manic at this moment, or that she was high, but it's also possible she had a good reason. My father gave everybody lots of good reasons to want to kill him. She gathered the edges of the towel up into a kind of sack, and together we ran down the street like thieves. At a sewer grate she stopped and kneeled, and I watched as she threw every single knife down the hole.

I write that now because it feels important. It feels necessary to illustrate the extremes to which my father drove people. When I sat down to write this, I knew I shouldn't make my father grotesque. And yet it would be very hard not to. He was not deep or thoughtful in any way. He never had many interests.

He used to sing, and his voice was technically perfect, but had no feeling, and eventually he dropped it. Instead, he painted really bad pictures of mountains and old barns, the kind that sell at craft shows, and he watched old Tarzan movies—the ones with Johnny Weissmuller are the ones he liked, not the ones with Ron Ely or Lex Barker or Elmo Lincoln or anybody else—and that's about it. Still, after every phone conversation with him, I hung up and said, 'Prick.' Or 'moron.' 'Asswipe.' 'Piece of shit sonofabitch.' Even though the conversation was perfectly civil. Our conversations were always perfectly civil. Cordial. Formal, even. The weather. Who he saw on the bus. Keep it light.

Before I started writing this, I called my mother. I thought she could tell me something about him that would make him seem more real, less hollow. I asked her if she thought he had an interior life. There was a big pause.

"Mother?"

"I'm thinking."

Another big pause.

"You were married to him for twelve years," I said. "If there was anything going on inside his head, surely you would know about it."

"You'd think so, wouldn't you?"

She thought some more, and we talked some more, and we considered and then rejected several more possibilities.

"Then what is it with him?" I asked.

"I think he's a predator."

This was not a revelation. It's a conversation my mother and I have had before. I always told her she was exaggerating, that my father never touched me. But in a twenty-three-minute conversation about my father, the following words had come up: Sociopath, cipher, predator, unformed personality, and schizophrenic. When I told my mother that my father never touched me, that was the truth. What I didn't admit is that he wanted to. I'd known it for as long as I could remember. He looked at me. And when he did touch me, even though it was never what could be called 'inappropriate,' I didn't like it. But I never told anybody.

Next, I called Stephen, my best friend and a former boyfriend. It was a source of conflict throughout our seven-year relationship, and continued to be so in our friendship, that I resent my father so much more than my mother, who, as far as Stephen was concerned, was much the worst of the two. My father, he thought, was boring and insensitive and a bit shallow and not very bright, but none of those things was a reason to hate somebody. He couldn't understand why I was so angry at him. For the first time in the twenty-five years we had known each other, I told him.

"Oh," he said when I had finished. "Now I understand."

I have a memory of sitting on my father's lap in the sea. I can feel his chest hair against my shoulder. I want to run away.

125

For my mother, marriage to my father must have been frustrating. They met when she answered an ad for a shampoo girl at his beauty shop. She was sixteen and he was thirty-two. They were completely mismatched. My mother is intelligent and curious, while my father was...not. He was also shallow, while she is contemplative. He seemed interested in her mainly for her looks. Looks were important to him. He bragged often that people told him in his youth he looked like Burt Lancaster. I'd like to believe it wasn't true, that he was full of shit. But when I look at old photographs, there's no denying it. He was the spitting image.

I sometimes blame my mother for inflicting my father on the family. On me.

"What were you thinking?" I say.

"Obviously I wasn't," she replies. "I wanted to get out of the house and your father had money."

Or at least what passed for having money in my family, which meant that he had a job and could spring for a decent night out at the Griswold Inn. All this was a big change from her childhood home, where they shared a Salisbury steak four ways at dinner and got an orange each for a Christmas present. I suppose my father, with his wavy hair and his tailored suits, seemed like a big step up for a Livermore. They married a few months after they met. My grandmother had to give permission because my mother was underage. The truth is, she couldn't think clearly about marrying my father because she was a child at the time. She was a victim of my father's

126

predation. Their marriage just passed for acceptable because she was close to being of age.

My mother reminded me during our conversation that, after my parents were divorced, when I went to live with my father, I used to bar my bedroom door before I went to sleep. I hadn't remembered that until she mentioned it. She knew this because my sister Jennifer told her. Jennifer, who had a different father and lived with my mother, spent the night with us about once a week. She watched as I dragged the dresser in front of the door and pulled at the knob to make sure the door couldn't be opened. Jennifer asked me why I did it, and I gave her some reason. I don't remember what it was, but apparently it strained credulity, even for a seven-year-old.

"That doesn't happen in a normal household," my mother said.

My mother called child protective services, and they sent a social worker out to the house. A man called Zegler, my mother said. I remember a man in a necktie and no coat, with a clipboard. My father sat in the wing chair, I sat in the rocker. I remember my father sat with his legs crossed, hands clasped over one knee, smiling at me. When Zegler got back to the office, he called my mother.

"He said that he couldn't substantiate anything but had a very uncomfortable feeling," she said. "He suggested that I take you and your brother and move out of state, as far away from your father as possible."

The social worker never came back, and neither the state nor my mother took me from my father. I do not reveal this out of anger at my father, at least not completely. I reveal it because it is another stressor many poor children face. Researchers have found that low socioeconomic status contributes to the risk of child sexual abuse. I certainly do not claim that all poor people are pedophiles. Children in wealthy families are also abused, but researchers have found that, in those cases, their wealthy parents very often use their status to evade inquiries.

When child abuse happens in poor families, what does it do to the child who is already under so many other kinds of stress? And what options do they have? Child social services agencies are straining beneath the sheer numbers of cases of abuse and neglect, and case workers usually have to prove bodily injury before the state will remove the child from a parent's custody. My mother had already either been manipulated into surrendering custody of me or traded me to my father for a house, depending on who you believe. She was not in a position to petition the state for custody now. Run, was the option the social worker gave my mother. Why, then, did my mother leave me with him? We were thirty minutes from the Rhode Island border. Why didn't she take my brother and me and leave the state? In fact, why had she let my father take custody of me at all? It's very likely because she was simply worn down. She had been poor too long, lived with undiagnosed bipolar too long, was beaten down too long. Even if she had the money to take us and flee, she simply didn't have the strength. That is one of the first things poverty takes.

One day my father beat me. I don't remember why. I can't imagine what a ten-year-old could do to receive such a beating. Not the spankings that were administered periodically, which were bad enough. He *beat* me. He threw me over his

128

knee, pulled down my trousers and underwear and beat my bare bottom. He did it with his bare hand. All his rage, all his fury he let loose into that beating. When it was finally over, he pulled my underwear and pants up and let me go. I tried to walk, but I fell because of the pain. He tried to pick me up, but I kicked and screamed and cursed him until he finally gave up and went into his room and closed the door. I lay on the floor on my side for a long time, crying.

When I felt I could, I got up and walked unsteadily to my room and closed the door. I lay on my bed on my side. It would be three days before I could lie on my bottom. It was summer vacation, so I didn't have to worry about sitting in a chair in school. My buttocks turned red, then blue-black. My father bought me ice cream. I did not eat it. The bruises stayed for weeks. For the rest of my childhood, it was there between us. Something I had on him. When he tried to discipline me, I would look at him hard. I would make my face a scowl. *I'll tell,* my face said. *I'll tell everything.*

I remember my father sitting in a lawn chair at a picnic for the fife and drum corps of which I was a member when I was nine. About fifty kids, aged nine to eighteen, stood around eating hot dogs and drinking Coke. I was standing with a friend by the drinks cooler.

"Look," she smirked.

I looked over at my father. His legs were spread wide. He wore cut-off jeans shorts. He wasn't wearing underwear. His penis was poking out through the open leg.

129

My father was a topic of conversation in the family, a source of mockery and derision. My brother Adam and I railed against his racism and joked about his temper. He used to get so angry, he'd grit his teeth and clench his fist and yell, 'Swine, dog's body!' We howled with laughter at his hypochondria and his miserliness. He made a will, even though there was no money, just a derelict 1973 Datsun 1200 coupe with the passenger floorboard rotted out so you could watch the pavement whizz past as we drove. Adam and I used to argue over who would get the Bacitracin and who would get the Band-Aids. I once called my father collect, my freshman year at college in New York City. He wouldn't accept the charges.

His sexuality was also discussed. I remember a woman he began to spend time with after my parents divorced. She was called Helen and she was about six feet tall with very large hands. Even at age nine I knew Helen wasn't biologically a woman. I overheard my maternal grandmother and my Aunt Joe discussing it.

"Don't you think somebody should tell him?" my grandmother said.

"Oh he knows, Jane, don't you think he knows?"

I would have liked it if my father was with Helen. I would have liked that he'd found somebody, had a normal adult relationship. But Helen didn't last.

My mother remembers this episode differently. Or maybe it's another person she is remembering. She says the woman's name was not Helen but Diane. My mother said she was a transsexual but my grandmother said she couldn't be because she had a business card. My mother looked at it. 'Certified Public Accountant,' it said, and, on a corner below, 'Piano Player.'

It was not only my family who seemed uncomfortable with my father. My father's friend Don came to visit one weekend. My father leaned over to whisper something to him, and Don pushed him away.

"Get away, Allen, you make me nervous."

If my father was gay, I would not have cared less. None of the family would have. They speculated about it, as though it had to be pinned down. But nobody ever mentioned children.

Well, that's not exactly true. The school sent a relative of mine to a counsellor when he was eleven or twelve. I don't know how long he saw this counsellor, and I didn't hear anything about it until years later. At some point, though, I saw a medical report. It said that he had been repeatedly molested by my father. This is not being gay. My father was not gay. I think he was a pedophile.

I have a memory of coming home from school. I am eleven, or maybe twelve. The screen door slams behind me because the hinge is broken. My father's car is in the parking lot, but it is quiet when I enter the house. I walk through the kitchen into

the living room. My father jumps up from the couch. He is naked. I didn't know you were home, he says, and streaks across the room and up the stairs to his bedroom. It occurs to me later that I made a lot of noise coming in. He must have heard me. Why did he wait until I came into the room and saw him before he left?

My parents divorced when I was seven or eight. After I was sent to live with my father, when he lost the business and we could no longer live in the back of his beauty shop, we moved into a series of successively smaller flats. He stopped working a few years later, and we went on welfare. He kicked me out, and I was glad to leave.

One day when I was about twenty-seven it struck me that I hadn't heard from my father in about a month. This was unusual. He was living in Florida and usually called once a week to 'see how I was doing.' Once I'd said I was fine, he would tell me about his sinus problems, his bad back, how much issue No. 1 of the Superman comics was currently worth (his mother had thrown his entire collection out while he was away in the Navy in 1945—all 375 issues—and he still hadn't forgiven her), and all about the latest battle he was waging against some neighbor or other. My father was always having a falling out with somebody, somebody who'd 'misunderstood' him or 'took something the wrong way.'

I was relieved that I'd been spared the calls for a month, though in the back of my mind I knew it meant something was wrong. I was hoping he'd died. I pictured him lying face down on the floor of his caravan like a crime-scene victim. In the kitchen, maybe, just after eating fried eggs. My father lying dead, undiscovered for weeks, as neighbors passed by outside, swam in the lake nearby, had cookouts. Flies would be buzzing against the dusty window screens, maggots seething inside the meaty caverns opening all over his body as it decayed, the stench of his decomposing flesh seeping into the couch cushions.

Then one day Adam called.

"Daddy's in jail." He was thirty-one years old and still called my father daddy. He still does now at age fifty-eight.

My father had been arrested, Adam said, for exposing himself to a group of adolescent girls on a beach in New Smyrna Beach, Florida. He had been in the county lock-up for a month. He hadn't called anybody until now because he was embarrassed, Adam said. Even now he didn't want me to know. "Don't tell Chrissy," he'd said.

"We can't leave him there, Chrissy. Somebody's gotta bail him out."

Adam couldn't do it, of course. He was just out of jail himself, had just finished a several-years-long stretch for some robbery or other. I can't remember the details. It's how he made his living for twenty years or so. The prison sentences all run together after a while.

We debated calling my Aunt Marilyn, but decided against it. We were squeamish enough just talking about it to each other. We had never talked about my father's—What? Predilections?—before. The thought of bringing in my father's sister—who had money, who lived in a tidy ranch house with her respectable husband and plastic covers on the furniture, who used to talk to our father in quiet tones in the next room about Adam's nascent stealing and my inadequate nutrition, was too humiliating. We agreed finally that I would call the jail and talk to my father, find out how much bail was, and make the arrangements.

I don't remember much about my conversation with my father. I know I asked him how much bail would be, and that it was around $1,000. I don't think we discussed why he was there. I know we never discussed it since.

I don't think he served any jail time beyond the month in the county lock-up. I know he was put on probation, though for how long I'm not sure. And I know that he was required to register as a sex offender and would be listed that way for the rest of his life, which meant, among other things, that he couldn't live within a certain distance of a school or playground and had to inform the police if he changed address.

It seems strange now, after everything I've written, because surely the things my father had done to me were done to *me* and were worth hating him for, that what I'm about to relate is the incident that keeps coming up when I think of my father and why I hate him.

It happened when we were living on Warner Street. 'When we were living on Warner Street' is shorthand in my family for 'before we moved to the projects.' I was about six, so that would make Adam about ten. It was around that time that he began stealing and exhibiting the other behaviors that prompted what happened next. It was Christmas Eve, and my father came home to tell us that Mrs. Zimmer, the wife of the captain of the Navy base and a client of his at the beauty shop, had invited us to Christmas dinner the next day. The Zimmers had money, so to my father, being invited to their house was an honor. He was bubbling with excitement, so Adam got excited, too. Christmas dinner at the Zimmers, won't that be great? My father said. Nice big house, and a big tree, and a beautiful table.

"There's just one thing," my father said. "She said Adam can't come."

I don't know how to describe my brother's face. If you could see the moment that changes somebody forever, the moment when everything falls apart, that was the look on Adam's face. It collapsed.

I can see it now. I see our family. I see everything we could have been, should have been, but are not. I see my brother, that happy little boy, and I see the man he is now. If you look at a photograph of him smiling, you can see it's not really a smile at all. He looks like he's crying. That is why this is the episode that makes me hate my father. He destroyed my brother's life, and he destroyed what our family could have been. Not just in this moment, in everything he did. Always making the cruel remark, the wrong decision, the choice that would increase ill will. And the predation. But, even at six years old, this was the moment that brought it all home to me.

All of this is unbelievable to me even now. But it is true. I wish I could give you more fine detail, but I can't. My memories of this period are very vague. Everything is sketchy. A flash here, a grainy image there. Then nothing. At least I'm being honest.

For the first time I am, to paraphrase Robert Lowell, saying what happened.

My mother thinks I'm not. She thinks that my father molested me and that I have repressed the memories. Is this why my memories are so dim? Somehow I don't think so. I went to therapy twice a week for five or six years. If it was there, I think they would have found it.

Just to be sure, I asked Stephen.

"I really don't think so, and I'll tell you why," he said. "I've had sex with you. You don't have any hang-ups."

It shocked me when he said it, and still bothered me when I got off the phone and for some time afterward. I spent several days trying to figure out why, and then it struck me: Trying to come to terms with my relationship with my father had triggered a conversation about my sexuality. That is humiliating. And that is what I've felt my whole life. Humiliated. Even though my father did not molest me, I feel as ashamed as if he had. I am ashamed that he wanted to. What is it about me? Why would my own father want to do that to me? I know the answer is that it has nothing to do with me. In an article about sex abuse in the Catholic Church for the Social Science Research Council, Steven Mintz wrote that Alfred Kinsey, in his study of female sexual behavior, reported that one-quarter of girls under the age of 14 reported having experienced sexual abuse.[3] And apparently fathers abusing their daughters is

---

[3] Mintz, Stephen. "Placing childhood sexual abuse in historical perspective." *Social Science Research Council*, 13 July 2012. tif.ssrc.org/2012/07/13/placing-childhood-sexual-abuse-in-historical-perspective/.

nothing new. Mintz wrote that the historian Lynn Sacco found some 500 newspaper articles about father–daughter incest between 1817 and 1899. But knowing that is not the same as being relieved of the shame. I feel shame for what people will think of me when they read this.

My father used to be more than six feet tall. At age 84, he is my height, just shy of 5' 8". He has lost height because of natural aging and because of the collapse of several discs in his back. His hair, what is left of it, is white and wispy, and his pink scalp shows through. He has lost much of his body weight. He is all bone. His cheeks are sunken. He wears big thick glasses that make his face all eyes, filmy with cataracts.

During a phone call he tells me that his long-time friend John is no longer speaking to him.

"I think it's that wife of his," he says. "Lori." He says her name as though it were somehow proof of bad character or mental infirmity.

It seems he had been to their house for dinner, where he had talked quite a bit with Lori's twelve-year-old daughter, and Lori had "taken it the wrong way."

"Oh well," he says. "That's the way it goes."

One should feel pity for somebody like this, a frail old man who sits alone in his senior citizen flat, two rooms and a bath with fluorescent lighting and institutional tile floors, ticking off the friends who no longer speak to him, watching Tarzan movies and listening to old radio episodes of Our Hit Parade. He must be so bewildered. He must wonder what happened to his life. Or at least I imagine that is what he thinks. And I do feel sorry for him, but in the way you would for a stranger. Then I remember he is my father, and what that means, and all I feel is revulsion.

He is also sick. He's had several heart attacks, and had a quadruple bypass and two stents put in his chest to prevent another. One year he has a stroke and the next year he develops colitis. He is in and out of the hospital monthly for bleeding because of the Coumadin he takes to prevent another stroke.

One day my brother called.

"Daddy's in the hospital."

All I could think is, Please let this be it.

He'd had a minor heart attack and had intestinal bleeding from the blood thinner.

"I want the Bacitracin," I said.

I heard Adam chuckle. "No, I want the Bacitracin. You can have the Band-Aids."

But my father wasn't dying. The doctors had stopped the intestinal bleed and inserted tubes into his nose to staunch more bleeding there. He was expected to be well enough to go home in a couple of days.

"This is getting ridiculous," Adam said. "Even the doctors are following him around saying, 'Enough already. Will you get in the box?'"

We talked about our father's health problems, and Adam reminded me that our father says his father used to beat him, sometimes until he passed out, and I felt a twinge of guilt for being so angry at him.

"Well, if there's a Jesus somewhere he's going to have to take us as we are or fucking not at all," Adam said.

After I finished talking to my brother, I called my father's hospital room. It rang for a long time. Finally, he picked up. He was crying. He had to go to the bathroom, and somebody had placed the call button out of reach. I hung up to call the nurses' station and tell them he needed help. I was glad I could do this small thing for him. I was also glad to be able to get off the phone. I am ashamed to be somebody who feels this way. I'm ashamed to be somebody who is disappointed after receiving word that her father is not dying. But that is how it is.

I began thinking about the ways in which my father's behavior affected me, and suddenly things that I didn't understand about myself began to make sense.

I dressed like a tomboy for many years. I realize now that this was not only because of what happened with Luis. It was to deflect my father's attention. When I was sixteen and got my first proper boyfriend, I wanted to dress like a girl but found I didn't know how. My friend Becky took me around to clothing shops, helped me pick out dresses and shoes, helped me figure out what looked good and what didn't.

I also found myself constantly worried that I wasn't feminine enough. It's a problem I still deal with now. How do you dress like a woman without appearing to invite unwanted sexual attention? More importantly, how feminine can you feel without sending a signal to men that you're vulnerable, that you can simply be taken? This conversation must now of course take place in the context of the #MeToo movement, but for me its roots are not in the men I have encountered outside my home but the one I encountered within it.

I look under the bed and in all the closets before I go to sleep, and I bar the door if it is possible to do so. Every night. I must also have some kind of light on or I can't fall asleep. I've tried sleeping in the dark, but I imagine that I see a figure in the corner of the room, just emerging from the shadows. I know he's not there. I tell myself he's not there, but it never works. My heart beats faster and I keep turning to check, and eventually I give up and switch on the nightlight.

On January 23, 2014, my father really did die. I was living in St Andrews in the United Kingdom, working on a PhD. The phone rang at one o'clock in the morning. It was my cousin Edward. He had my father's power of attorney and had been looking after my father and his affairs. When I saw what time it was I knew why he was calling, because Edward would not call me at one in the morning for any other reason, and as I saw his name on the caller ID and checked the time I said, "Oh thank God."

He sounded sad. Edward loved my father. He didn't know anything of what my father had done, or maybe he'd heard things and didn't believe them, or maybe he believed them and found the grace to love my father anyway. I'm not sure. I have never discussed it with him. I haven't wanted to ruin my father's image for him. I hope he never reads this. But he knew there were things between my father and me, things that made me stay away, and he seemed to understand, I think, that you can never know what goes on in a family.

He told me that my father's passing had been peaceful, and that he was sorry for my loss, and we talked about his family and mine, and how strange life was.

"Are you coming home for the funeral?" he asked after a while. "I'm not judging you at all. I just need to know for the arrangements."

I told him I was not. I didn't have the money for the flight, I said. This was a lie. I just could not bring myself to go.

After I hung up, I wandered around the flat, tidying my desk. I looked out the window. Black beyond. The pond that lay beneath my window was out there, I knew, but I couldn't see it in the dark moonless night. Only the pond, I told myself. Nothing more. The dark hours in Scotland can feel uncanny. Birds sing at night. Shapes hulk and shift in the haar. I went to bed and slept with the television on. I dozed on and off, and at three I woke, heart pounding. I was sure he was in the room. Don't be ridiculous, I thought.

I lay still, trying to fall back to sleep. After a while I got up, gathered blankets and shirts and coats and covered all the mirrors in the flat. I knew in my head this was an ancient practice. People feared that if the dead saw themselves in a mirror they would not cross over into the realm of the afterlife and would remain to haunt them. In my heart, that wasn't too far from the truth. I was afraid I would see my father in the mirror. I was afraid he would see me. Now that he was dead, unmoored from his body, could he get me?

The next morning I called Stephen, just to let him know. He was at work in Edinburgh, where he lived, an hour away.

"Should I come down there?"

"No, it's all right. I'm fine."

I hung up, then grew frightened again, and called back. "You'd better come."

"I'm already on my way," he said.

He arrived about ninety minutes later. We walked into town, the three medieval streets where food and drink and groceries were to be had, got lunch at a pub we liked, then went to the market and stocked up on groceries so we could hole up in the flat for a few days and do whatever it is one does in a situation like this. We really didn't know. At the end cap of one aisle, I spotted a display basket overflowing with packages of blueberry muffins. They looked like the kind we got when I was a child, the kind that taste like high fructose corn syrup. They were dotted with what I knew were freeze-dried blueberries

142

and shone with a slick patina. I bought them, insisting they had apotropaic properties. They could ward off the dead.

We returned to the flat and ate the apotropaic muffins and ordered in pizza for dinner. Stephen made up a song, set to the tune of 'Bloody Mary' from the musical South Pacific, composed primarily of the words "Christian's father was a pedo fuck."

I know this sounds disrespectful, appalling. But neither of us knew how to act, what to do, and it was Stephen's way of expressing the anger he felt at my father for making me feel so unsafe, stalked, like prey.

My sister Jennifer, I knew, was sitting shiva for my father in his hospital room until the undertaker could arrange to carry him to the mortuary. She was not his daughter, she had a different father, but she knew Edward would want it, so she volunteered to do it. My father had denied his Jewishness his entire life but became superficially enamored of it near the end and decided he wanted a Jewish burial. Within the first twenty-four hours this became impossible, or at least that part of it, because state law required certain paperwork, the signature of the coroner, and other necessities. All routine but time-consuming. His funeral was delayed further because the rabbi wasn't available until the following Tuesday, having services to perform for members of the synagogue. He was also barred from the Jewish cemetery, quite properly, because he was not a member, having refused to pay the membership fee. He had not in fact been to the synagogue since he was a boy and had not called himself a Jew for more than seventy years. In the end, the only thing Jewish about his service was that it was conducted by a rabbi.

The funeral was sparsely attended. I try to think this is because my father was old and most of the people he knew had died. But then my Uncle David died. The wake lasted two hours and the queue to pay respects at the coffin never slowed.

"How sad that is," Stephen said later of my father. "To have lived an entire life and made such a small mark on the world."

Sad. Yes. Sad for my father, sad for us. For the mark he did not make, for the marks he did.

I don't know how to end this. I don't know if I should be telling it. It's rank and foul and drags private shameful things into the open. It may hurt people. I've been shaking as I write it. I don't know if that's a sign I should stop, or a sign I should keep going. I do know I can no longer justify not telling it, for not telling is how such things are allowed to keep happening.

My mother reminds us all repeatedly that holding a grudge is like swallowing poison and expecting the other person to die. I still wonder sometimes at my failure to feel sadness at my father's death, whether this is righteous anger or the kind of grudge my mother warns against, or whether I am a bad person.

The Tuesday after my father died, in fact while his funeral was underway, I attended the creative writing class for which I served as a teaching assistant to my creative PhD supervisor.

"I wasn't sure you were going to turn up today," he said.

After class, as we discussed how I seemed 'fine' and the fact that I wasn't attending the funeral, I tried to justify my decision with a sentence Stephen and I had spent the weekend crafting, something that didn't expose the ugly details but delivered the essence of my reason for failing to fulfil my filial mourning obligations. "My father was a brutal man."

My supervisor took this in, and I watched him try to form an equally crafted sentence, one that acknowledged what I'd said but, I think, gave me permission to be sad anyway. "You still have to grieve."

"I don't know," I said. "Do you?"

THE POOR BODY

I am 32 years old. I am having trouble climbing the stairs. I'm not winded and I'm not overweight; I work out five times a week, lift weights three times a week and do the treadmill an hour a day. I simply can't lift my body onto the next step. There are cement blocks tied to my legs. I climb one step and stop. I wait, find the strength to lift my other leg. I haul myself up another step.

Waking up hurts. I have always slept badly, but now I can't lift my body from the bed, my eyes burn, I'm not sure where I am. A counsellor once told me that when two people in love break up, the energy field that envelops them tears as they are ripped apart. Waking up feels like that. *Waking me* is torn from *sleeping me*, and I want to weep, sometimes do weep. I am freelancing and don't have health insurance. I live with it.

I have been through many jobs since I graduated college, and my inability to sleep got me fired from many of them. When I graduate in 1991, I take a job as an editorial assistant at Bantam Doubleday Dell. My salary is $19,000 a year. I still can't sleep so I come in late pretty much every day. One day my boss calls me into her office. That is never good, and with her it is always even worse. No one in the office likes this woman. She is unkind and says cruel things to people and goes through assistants on a regular basis. I am her third assistant that year. It is May. The editorial assistants are sitting around one day on our lunch hour looking through a book of baby names, I don't remember why, and somebody says to look up my boss's name.

"It means consecrated to God," the girl with the book says.

I scoff. "Does it say when?"

Anyway, as I expected, when I go into my boss's office, she fires me for routine tardiness.

Because of the recession, my boyfriend has not been earning much money, either, and now I am unemployed, so it is at this time that we move to Connecticut and stay with my mother while we try to get on our feet.

I get a job at a government contractor. I come in late because I can't sleep. I get fired.

I get a job somewhere else; I don't even remember now where it was. I still can't sleep, but rather than tell people I can't sleep, I call in sick a lot. I invent illnesses. Because I am tired of telling people that I have only slept two, three, four hours. Don't know how to explain to them that I can't sleep, and make them understand why, so they don't say "You need to stop partying and go to bed earlier, you're not in college anymore."

After losing several jobs in Connecticut and breaking up with my boyfriend, I decide to move back to New York, where work is at least more plentiful. I decide to freelance. I figure I can work when I can function and take days off when I haven't slept. This works pretty well; I even get a long-term evening gig proofreading for a tech startup, which means I don't have to worry about oversleeping. I work 4pm to midnight, and I stop at the Vietnamese restaurant on Canal Street and order a giant Vietnamese iced coffee and nurse it throughout my shift. The only problem is that I don't have health insurance. But I am one of the 'young invincibles,' the twenty-somethings who think they don't need health insurance because they're young and healthy. I don't even consider my lifelong insomnia a health problem. It is just who I am. I am a person who doesn't sleep.

The tech startup goes out of business, and I decide to go back to regular jobs. In addition to health insurance, the job has dental insurance, the first time I have had it since I stopped being on state aid at age 18. I see the dentist for the first time in seven years. He tells me I have gum disease.

I get a job as a technical writer. I come in late because I can't sleep. Before I can be fired, the Towers fall. I am laid off.

I move to Georgia to get my baby sister away from the unhealthy environment she has been in. I get a full-time job and crappy health insurance. I go to a GP and say I can't sleep. He does a blood test and says I'm fine.

"I'm exhausted," I tell him. "Cripplingly exhausted."

There are more tests he could run, but my insurance won't cover it. He smiles and tells me to see the nurse on my way out. That is to pay my co-pay.

My bones begin to hurt. I get a better job and better health insurance and a better doctor. She runs the tests my previous insurance wouldn't pay for. She calls me the next day at work. Not only do I have thyroid disease, but I also have parathyroid disease. I don't even know what that second one is. She prescribes Synthroid and sends me to an endocrinologist. I have two visits with him, but then I get offered a job in New York and I take it.

I move back to New York and start the job and have even better health insurance. I am going to take advantage of this Cadillac health insurance while I have it. I tell my new GP that I can't sleep and that my doctor in Georgia diagnosed me with thyroid disease and hyperparathyroidism. He sends me to an endocrinologist. The endocrinologist medicates me for the thyroid disease and sends me to a surgeon at Mt. Sinai for the parathyroid disease. He is one of the leading surgeons in his field. In 2006 he performed the first jaw transplant using the patient's jaw and bone marrow. He takes my blood and tells me my calcium is very high. That is how parathyroid disease damages the body. As the Mayo Clinic explains in its online page on the subject: Parathyroid glands maintain appropriate levels of calcium and phosphorus in the blood by turning the secretion of parathyroid hormone (PTH) on or off. "When calcium levels in your blood fall too low, your parathyroid glands secrete enough PTH to restore the balance. PTH raises calcium levels by releasing calcium from your bones and increasing the amount of calcium absorbed from your small intestine." But sometimes one of the glands (or more than one) releases too much PTH. That is how it damages the body. One or more glands misreads your levels and thinks you are low on calcium, so it leaches it from your bones and pumps it into your bloodstream, along with excess phosphorous. This can cause kidney stones, osteoporosis, excessive urination, abdominal pain, tiring easily or weakness, depression or forgetfulness, bone or joint pain, frequent complaints of illness with no apparent cause, nausea, vomiting and loss of appetite. I had every symptom but one. No osteoporosis. "Moans, groans, kidney stones, and psychiatric overtones" was the mnemonic my new GP said they taught them in med school in order to remember it so they could diagnose it when they saw it.

The surgeon schedules a series of tests to try to determine which gland is causing the problem so he can get in and out fast. The shorter the surgery, the better for the patient. For one of them I sit on the machine and huge boxes attached to the machine with steel arms whirl around my head and neck. Then he tries something else, and then something else. One after one, the tests come up empty. A week before the surgery, he tries one last time to determine which gland is causing the problem, an invasive procedure called parathyroid venous catheterization. They did it on an outpatient basis at Mt Sinai. A radiologist made a small incision and inserted a catheter into the vein in my groin. Then he threaded the catheter up through my body and chest and into my neck. In the recovery room, I was hungry. I had been made to fast before the test, so I hadn't had anything all day and it was nearing 5pm.

"You're hungry?" he said. "I'll go get you something."

I assumed he was going to run up to the hospital cafeteria. He came back shortly with a turkey sandwich wrapped in clingfilm. I was a vegetarian, but I thanked him and ate it. I didn't notice it at the time because I was still groggy from whatever they had given me for the procedure, but it struck me that evening that the sandwich didn't look like the kind they give you in hospitals. It was wrapped differently, and the turkey was real. He had given me his own dinner. What a nice man, I thought, and I wished I had known at the time so I could refuse to take his dinner from him, or to thank him if he insisted. He is one of the people who helped me to understand that not everybody wants to hurt you. A lot of people want to be nice. It's important to remember these people and to acknowledge them. They are what gets us all through.

At my next appointment with the surgeon, he tells me that that test didn't find anything either.

"Well, we'll just have to go in and find the sucker the old-fashioned way," he said.

On the day of the surgery he opens me up and immediately sees a gland that is significantly larger than the rest. He takes it out and does a PTH assay. My PTH levels have dropped to normal levels.

"It was huge," he says of the gland when he visits me in the recovery room. "There was no missing it."

I stare at my throat in the bathroom mirror that night. An angry wound, a horizontal line about an inch long, is slashed across the flesh. Covered with surgical tape it looks milky and swollen, as though something is trying to push its way out. I feel the instinctive need to run, that I have been attacked by something and gravely injured, but I know this is an ancient fear from another age when animals stalked us, so I switch off the bathroom light and go to bed.

Once I recover from the initial trauma of the surgery I feel instantly better. It took ten years.

But I am still tired because I still cannot sleep. Until finding this current job I have been hired and let go from a number of jobs by now, not because my work is not good—it is, they love me—but because I cannot get to work on time. Just as it has been my entire life, I lie in bed watching the clock tick over, three o'clock, four o'clock, five o'clock, and sometimes I manage to rise from my bed and make it to the office, but never on time, and sometimes I am not able to rise from my bed because I haven't slept at all, and I call in sick. I get fired—laid off, they call it, because my work is outstanding and they don't want to hurt my chances at getting another job—I get another job, and I get fired again.

Since this latest job comes with such great health insurance, and since I have managed not to get fired and I want to keep it that way, I ask my GP if my insurance will pay for a sleep specialist. It will, at least mostly. I will have to pay a couple of hundred dollars, but I will worry about that later. My GP refers me to this sleep specialist. His given name is Alcibiades, and in my mind, I draw parallels of greatness with the famous Athenian statesman who is his namesake. The sleep specialist orders a battery of bloodwork and a sleep study. I turn up at 7pm on a Friday night on the East Side of Manhattan and the technologist affixes dozens of sensors to my head and chest and back, and wraps me in a cage and crown of wires, and I sleep, or rather I don't sleep, and the technologist monitors my not-sleeping from the next room.

At my next appointment, the sleep specialist tells me that I have a melatonin deficiency and my circadian rhythm is off. My body simply doesn't produce enough melatonin, and there's nothing that can change that, so I must take tablets under my tongue about half an hour before bedtime. To normalize my circadian rhythm, I must stand in the sunlight for 15 minutes every morning on waking, get as much sunlight as possible during the day, and wear sunglasses outside after 3pm to signal to my body that it is time to start winding down. I must do this for the rest of my life. That's fine, I say. I'll do anything if it helps me sleep.

"I'm sorry we couldn't help you before this," he says. "It turns out your problems are so simple to fix, but sleep science is just now getting to a place where we know these things."

I'm just grateful to find a solution after all these years, I say. I wouldn't have had the health insurance for the test before now anyway, I think.

"What did you do before this?" he said.

"Got fired a lot."

He winces and looks away, and I fight the tears rising in my eyes at his kindness.

I go to GNC and buy the melatonin tablets he's told me to get, and I emerge into the bright sunlight of Second Avenue and put on my sunglasses. It is 3:30pm.

At eleven that night, I put two melatonin tablets under my tongue and climb into my bed and stare out at Storm King mountain standing black against the indigo sky. The last time I look at the clock, it is 11:30. And then I am asleep.

I wake at 7:30am with no alarm. I lie in bed a moment, not quite believing. I am awake. I am rested. I get out of bed. I go to the kitchen, get my coffee and stand in the square of sunlight in my kitchen window, watching the breeze brush the trees. And I cry with relief.

But my bones still hurt. I live with it awhile, out of habit, I suppose. Americans are used to not seeking treatment unless the need is dire. But the pain is becoming more and more intense. Sometimes it is as though somebody is sawing at my hip bones with a blade, and sometimes they are digging the point of the blade into the acetabulum, where the hip meets the femur. My fingers are beginning to stiffen and ache and burn. I feel them tighten when I make a fist. I worry that the parathyroid disease has returned, so after a few months I tell my endocrinologist. He orders a CT scan and a bone density scan and some other scan, the name of which I can't remember, because I have excellent health insurance and it will pay. All the scans are negative. You're fine, he tells me. My bones still hurt.

I get accepted into a master's program at the University of St. Andrews in Scotland. The week before I leave for the UK, I break my big toe. I've left my job to pack and don't have health insurance. I email my GP. He tells me to tape my big toe to my second toe, so that's what I do.

I move to the UK. Now my toe hurts, too. I go to NHS Scotland. Maybe a break that didn't heal right? I ask my doctor. He takes an X-ray.

"Your toe healed okay," Dr. Wills says. "That pain you're feeling is the arthritis."

"What arthritis?" I say.

"Your arthritis," he says.

"I don't have arthritis," I say.

He looks at me like he's almost amused, then he sees I truly didn't know and he looks at me the same way the sleep specialist did. These doctors are in a university town, a university at which 16 percent of the students are American. The doctors who treat them probably see the consequences of the American healthcare system all the time.

"Did nobody ever tell you that you have arthritis?"

I look at him like either he's crazy or I am.

"It's pretty far along," he says. "I would say advanced severe arthritis. I would say you've had it for six or seven years."

The doctors in the States didn't find my arthritis because they didn't listen to me. They did all the expensive tests they could do because they got paid a lot for them. When none of those tests worked, they had made all the money they could make on the problem. It simply never occurred to anybody to take an X-ray. It took an NHS doctor to think to start with a simple X-ray and find out what the problem was, because there is no profit motive in the NHS because it is nationalized healthcare. They are motivated to keep you healthy because letting you get sick is expensive, and those costs will be paid by the state, which means by the taxpayers.

Dr. Wills never tells me I'm fine. He treats my arthritis and my thyroid disease and later my menopause. He monitors me diligently and tests me regularly, and one time he does have to order every expensive test in the book to find out what is wrong, and when one of the tests establishes that the arthritis is actually rheumatoid arthritis; he treats that, too. Eventually, most likely very soon, I will need both hips and both knees replaced. That will be four surgeries, followed with months of physical rehabilitation after each.

That I have rheumatoid arthritis is particularly interesting in a discussion about the consequences of poverty. Many studies have found a link between childhood trauma or stress and illness as an adult. Anxiety provokes the body's stress response. Your body produces more adrenaline, your heart races, your body primes itself to react. This chronic stress causes inflammation, and the inflammation leads to a whole host of health problems. Cardiovascular disease, autoimmune diseases, like thyroid disease and parathyroid disease and osteoarthritis and rheumatoid arthritis. Having rheumatoid arthritis also doubles my risk for heart attack. A 2021 study of Generation X adults born in 1970 found that those who grew up in poorer families were 43% more likely to have multiple long-term health conditions than their peers from wealthier households.[4]

It's not just chronic physical illnesses that plague people who grew up poor. They also have greater incidences of mental health problems: Anxiety, depression, bipolar. Indeed, schizophrenia is much more prevalent in poor people. A person can have the gene for schizophrenia, but if they are brought up in a stable home the gene won't necessarily get turned on. If a person grew up in poverty, that gene is more likely to be activated.

I am lucky. Rheumatoid arthritis is considered a manageable condition in the United Kingdom, and as it progressed, I was able to work less and less, but I still got the care I needed

---

[4] The Guardian, https://www.theguardian.com/society/2021/jul/28/a-third-of-middle-aged-uk-adults-have-at-least-two-chronic-health-issues-study

because healthcare in the UK is not linked to employment as it is in the United States. In the United States I would have to be considered completely disabled to get the insurance necessary to treat the disease. If you have a chronic illness in the United States, you are made to feel like a burden on taxpayers. And if you do get on Medicaid, people resent you. The lack of universal healthcare and a social safety net has ground Americans down, and they are tired and they are angry, so the suggestion that everybody should put some of their money into a pot for it to be shared out amongst the entire population creates stress, anxiety and anger, and the results are barbaric and inhumane.

At my last job before I left the States, at a newspaper in the Hudson Valley, I got a call from a man called Andrew Pacini. He had stage 4 pancreatic cancer and no health insurance. When he was diagnosed, he told his boss at the factory he'd worked at for many years, and they deemed him unfit to work and laid him off. When he lost his job, he also lost his health insurance, of course, because this is America, and he couldn't afford COBRA. He applied for Medicaid, but because he worked the previous year, which is how they determine benefits, he wasn't eligible. As part of the story I was writing, I called the Medicaid representative. He confirmed the details Andrew had given me and said there was nothing he could do. I could tell that he was crying.

A few weeks after the first story ran, Andrew Pacini was rushed to the hospital in excruciating pain. They stabilized him and sent him home and told him to follow up with his GP. No painkillers, no hospice.

He died.

GOODBYE TO YOU

I have a terror of flying that is difficult to describe. Whenever I get on a plane, I am certain that I will be dead within hours. It is not a fear; it is absolute conviction. I mentally take my leave of friends and family as I wait in the departures lounge. I think of all the things I will not have the opportunity to do. I am pathetic and inconsolable. But all my life I dreamed of moving to Europe. This was a preposterous notion for a girl growing up in the projects. Just graduating high school was an accomplishment; college and a job were success beyond the wildest dreams of society and its expectations for people like me. Europe was another world.

When I learned that I'd been awarded a place in the MLitt in Creative Writing program at the University of St Andrews, I considered booking passage on a cruise ship, but it was too expensive. I even consulted a world map to investigate a land route. It turns out I could take the train to Alaska, then board a boat at the Seward Peninsula and cross the Bering Strait to Russia. From there I could make my way to Vladivostok and hop the Trans-Siberian Railway to Moscow, then catch the Moscow–Paris Express, change to the Eurostar from Paris to London, then hop a train at London King's Cross to Edinburgh and on to St. Andrews. It was only with great regret that I admitted to myself how impractical this was and decided to fly. On my last visit to my doctor before my health insurance was cancelled, I got a prescription for Xanax to take on the flight.

At the airport I wept, from the fear of the flight but also with regret at leaving my family behind. My niece Lily, barely two, had fallen asleep during the drive to the airport, I didn't even get to say goodbye properly. Shortly after she was born, my sister Charity drove from Connecticut to the Hudson Valley so I could meet the baby, and we drove with my mother and brother-in-law to the behemoth shopping outlet near my apartment. Lily sat next to me in her car seat in the back of the Murano, and she studied me with an intensity I have never seen before or since. I looked back at her and let her take the measure of me. We bonded during that car ride, and she has been my little BFF ever since.

"Bye, Lil," I said at the airport, leaning into the car to kiss her sweaty baby forehead, her eyebrows turned down in a frown as toddlers' sometimes do when they fall asleep without wanting to.

My sister walked me into the departures lounge.

"You're doing the right thing," she said, hugging me.

After I went through security, I bought a bottle of water and took a Xanax. As they called my flight, I took another. I found my seat and stowed my carry-on in the overhead, buckled myself in and took an Ambien.

I had successfully drugged myself to the degree that I remember little of the flight. I vaguely remember chatting with the young man next to me about our reasons for the trip. He was heading off to grad school somewhere as well, but I don't remember where or what he would be studying. He seemed perfectly comfortable with the idea that I, too, had been accepted to study at an elite institution abroad, and I noted with surprise that he didn't seem to be thinking to himself, *poor white trash.*

When we landed in London, I dropped my suitcases at the hostel and went directly to St. Paul's Cathedral a block away. I stood outside and took a photo of myself. In the photo, my hair is frizzy, I have dark circles under my eyes, and I am the happiest I have ever been in my life. I have the madness in my eyes of the escaped lunatic. I spent the afternoon in the cathedral, climbed Christopher Wren's great dome and, although I am not a believer, sat in the choir for Evensong. Later, I walked along the Thames to Westminster and sat on a bench in the twilight. Cleopatra's Needle stood steel grey against the river, the shrapnel marks from a bomb dropped by German Gotha bombers invisible in the fading light. Many years before, I had seen its twin in Central Park and read that the other was in London and thought, I wish I could see that.

A very old man hobbled along, leaning heavily on a cane. He paused to rest and smiled softly at me, seeming to wonder if he should approach. I smiled back, and he came and lowered himself in the creaky way of old men onto the bench beside me. His accent was Yorkshire, with rounded vowels like he had marbles in his mouth and had learned how to speak around them.

"Thou art a long way from home," he said when he heard my accent.

I felt a rush of delight. He still said 'thy' and 'thou.' I learned later that this was a linguistic style particular to Yorkshire. He was old, but his back was straight, his hands resting on the tip of his cane as if in prayer, his eyes merry as he heard my story and told me his.

Two summers after I arrived, I finally went to the Continent. As always, I was broke, but I did have enough for a train ticket, so my friend and I booked our tickets and found a cheap hostel and went. From America, this trip would have been unthinkable. A flight would have been five hundred dollars at least. The train ticket was £78. The hostel was £80 apiece. For my spending money, I cashed in the change I had been saving for two years in an old milk jug. The entire trip would cost me £275.

We alighted at King's Cross and were hit with an almost solid mass of air at least 15 degrees warmer than Scotland, air that felt fizzy with possibility. At St. Pancras, we ate croissants and drank cappuccino in the early morning while we waited for our train to be announced. Around us, people spoke in English, French, German, Italian. The announcer invited us to board, and we climbed a steep ramp onto the platform, boarded the train and found our seats. The conductor welcomed us in English, French, German and Dutch as the train pulled away from the station. She told us that the train would rock gently from side to side as it reached its travelling speed of 160 kilometers an hour and that this was perfectly normal, not to worry.

For about an hour and a half, we passed through grey industrial towns and between concrete noise barriers, then the train dipped beneath the earth outside of Folkestone, and for twenty minutes we sped through the darkness of the Channel Tunnel. Stephen looked at his phone. I watched the intermittent lights of the tunnel fly past. Then, there was a barely perceptible upward trajectory, and the train broke into daylight. We sped past a road sign too quickly for me to read it, but it was in French. I looked out across fields of barley and wheat stretching in every direction, and in the distance, I saw a small white country church, and I cried.

I moved to Scotland, and have visited London and Paris, Ireland and Wales, the Netherlands, Berlin and Bruges and Ghent, Poland and the Czech Republic. I rode a boat through the canals in Amsterdam and gazed upon Rembrandt's The Night Watch. In Kraków, I nearly broke a washing machine; the drum was closed, and I thought it somehow worked by rolling the clothes around the outside of the drum like an old-fashioned washboard. They still had those kinds of things in Europe, didn't they? I passed beneath the horrible gate at Auschwitz, with its cruel slogan Arbeit Macht Frei (work makes you free) emblazoned across the top in iron, and bowed my head before the murdered dead. Standing on the Charles Bridge in Prague, my childhood seemed a world away. But a part of me is still that little girl in the projects eating government cheese and fighting to protect my own body. I am not only that girl, but she is always there, waiting to be buffeted by a memory, to be cowed by shame.

I am lucky. Many Americans like me, most of them, will not be able to do the things I have been able to do. Even many middle-class Americans will not be able to afford even one trip to Europe in their lives. It was only with enormous good fortune that I was able to, and a staggering amount of student loan debt. I gave up a lot. I ran away to Europe, but I also ran away from something. From my country, from who I thought I was there, who other people thought I was, and who I thought they believed me to be. You lose things when you run, too. You lose quotidian experiences with your family, the kind of face time that deepens friendships, and the simple connections that make you feel like you have a home place. The farther you run, the harder it is to return. Whether you think you want to or not, an inability to return home is a lonely feeling.

I had to leave America before I could write about it. I had to get the voices out of my head. The voices are persistent and insidious. Even now, I seem unable to write about the projects in fiction. That part of me is, so far, reserved for essays. It is as though I am two people: The girl before the projects and the girl after.

When you return to the States after an extended period abroad, you see it more through the eyes of an outsider, and the view is shocking. When I went back to visit after my first year in Scotland, as people spoke, I thought, 'Why is everyone yelling?' Americans are *loud*. I've always heard it said, but you don't realize it until you don't hear it for a while, until you don't have to shout to be heard. They are shouting to be heard, too, but nobody ever quite hears them. I listened to Americans who have never been to Europe pontificate to me about how much better everything is in America, and I sigh and feel angry at them and feel sympathy for them.

I think it was Edmund Burke who spoke of patriotism as a love of the landscapes of home, and when I think of America now, it is the landscapes I yearn for. Whenever I return, I search everywhere for familiar scenes. I love driving down the leafy roads outside the town in which my sister lives, not too far from where we grew up. I love sitting for hours by Bethesda Fountain in New York City, watching people come and go, living out the tiny dramas of their lives. I love driving down Victory Drive in Savannah towards Tybee Island, a canopy of live oaks joining hands above me, Spanish moss fluttering in the breeze like washing on the line. I love these times and these places, but they never quite feel like home.

When I returned to the States for what I thought was for good, I returned with a more European sensibility, and I panicked. 'Christ, I have no health insurance,' I thought. 'And Jesus, they've got guns.' *They've* got guns. *They* no longer included me. I was no longer one of them. And then I realized, I'm poor white trash; I never really was.

BRIDGE 2

I am 48. I have gone to grad school to pursue my dreams. In America, you can be anything. I have fallen for this before.

Grad school is too expensive in the States, so I went in the UK. I had wanted to do that my entire life anyway.

I got a master's. I got a PhD. I graduated in June. In August, I got a job. The job required a British or an EU passport. I didn't have a British passport, and I couldn't get the EU passport I'm entitled to because of my grandfather's birthplace as I lacked the funds I needed for the lawyer to apply. I couldn't get the passport for want of money. I lost the job for want of a passport.

I watch younger people with the right passport sail past me into jobs. I get a book contract. I watch younger people without book contracts but the right passport sail past me into jobs.

I apply for more than 100 jobs in the States. I don't get a job. I am too old, I don't have enough publications, I don't have the right publications, I am overqualified, I am underqualified, my doctorate is British, my references are British.

I move home and sleep in my mother's closet on beach chair cushions on the floor. Late one night I look up. Two cockroaches are crawling past my head. I scream, jump up, mash the roaches with a shoe. I have no place else to sleep. I lie back down.

I am right back where I started.

I get another book contract. Younger people without book contracts but the right credentials or the right passport or the right publications still sail past me into jobs.

I am 52. I'm broke. I owe $206,000 in student loans. And I am tired.

ALL COME TO LOOK
FOR AMERICA

"Let me tell you the truth. The truth is what is. And what should be is a fantasy, a terrible, terrible lie that someone gave the people long ago."

— Lenny Bruce

Simon and Garfunkel stood beneath a pale spotlight on the darkened stage of the David Letterman show. It was a YouTube video of a 2003 performance, posted by a friend on Facebook. The pair were about to embark on their reunion tour and were making the publicity rounds. The plaintive strains of Simon's guitar began, and they sang the first lines of 'America.' Without warning, I burst into tears. Desperate weeping that felt like I was dying. And as they sang the words 'All come to look for America...' I realized why. I've been looking for America all my life, but it's not there anymore. I'm not sure it ever was.

I was surprised that people were surprised Donald Trump won in 2016. To me, his election was inevitable. It was the culmination of years of economic anxiety, plummeting standards of living and the dulling of critical thinking. And racism. God knows, virulent, violent, American racism. Four years later and things are even worse than we could have imagined. Shocking numbers of people have emerged from the shadows, full of hate. We have become a raging cauldron, and on January 6, 2021 those people stormed the Capitol in an attempted coup to maintain Donald Trump, the man who lost the election, in power. We stand now on the brink of authoritarianism. In four short years. It happened so quickly, we say. But in reality, it happened over years and years, over decades. The tide was rolled back that day, but the insurrectionists wait, biding their time, gathering strength, so that they can return and try again. And next time, they may succeed.

How do we come back from this? As bad as it all is, what Trump and the Republican Congress did, policies can be fixed. The Muslim travel ban has been overturned, the boundaries of the Bears Ears National Monument have been restored, the tax bill can hopefully be repealed. But how do we fix *us*? How do we re-knit the fabric of our social cohesion? Our fellow Americans are diminished in our eyes. How do we regain some sense of common identity? How do we readmit them to the dinner table? How do we purge from our minds the images of white supremacists' torches snaking in an unholy line through the darkened streets of Charleston? How do we reconcile with the 68 percent of white Alabamans who voted for an alleged child molester rather than a district attorney who prosecuted Ku Klux Klan members who murdered four African American children? How do we forgive the people who saw Donald Trump separating children from their parents and putting little kids in cages and thought, Yes, that's right. People who, at a bare minimum, weren't horrified by it.

America was supposed to mean something. At the founding, we declared that meaning, those values to which we were committing ourselves as a nation: Equality, freedom, justice, domestic tranquility and ensuring the general welfare of our people. But truth be told, money has always been more important to us. It has become so important that we have stopped asking the questions essential to a good society, indeed to the American ideal, as Tony Judt said in *Ill Fares the Land*: "For thirty years we have made a virtue out of the pursuit of material self-interest: indeed, this very pursuit now constitutes whatever remains of our sense of collective purpose. We know what things cost but have no idea what they are worth. We no longer ask of a judicial ruling or a legislative act: is it good? Is it fair? Is it just? Is it right? Will it help bring about a better society or a better world?"

How did we come to be this way? We had such high hopes for ourselves, such lofty principles to which we committed the nation. The answer is right there in the Constitution, in which we asserted that a slave only counted as three-fifths of a human being. That willingness to suspend our commitment to liberty when money was involved was a declaration of our true values. In the last 100 years at least, money has become the rubric by which we direct our lives, our pursuits and our goals, the means by which we reckon success, even human value. Somehow, somewhere, we went desperately off course. We are sick at heart, and I don't know quite how it happened or how it can be fixed.

After the terrorist attacks of September 11[th,] the drumbeat for war began, and the United States invaded Afghanistan. Most New Yorkers I knew were against it. We thought there had been enough killing, and we couldn't see how carpet-bombing Afghanistan would help capture Osama Bin Laden, who was hiding in a cave somewhere, safe from the bombs falling outside. We also reckoned it had more to do with the pipeline a consortium of American oil companies wanted to run through Afghanistan than it did with Osama Bin Laden.

Surely this is one of the things that has eroded my America: the proliferation of foreign wars. President Dwight D. Eisenhower warned of this in his farewell address. He spoke of the growing power of the military–industrial complex and the pursuit of profit that would lead the industrial sector to foment military action in order to sell weapons and make money. "The total influence—economic, political, even spiritual—is felt in every city, every statehouse, every office of the federal government," he said. "We must not fail to comprehend its grave implications. Our toil, resources and livelihood are all involved. So is the very structure of our society. In the councils of government, we must guard against the acquisition of unwarranted influence, whether sought or unsought, by the military–industrial complex. The potential for the disastrous rise of misplaced power exists, and will persist."[5]

As Eisenhower warned, money that could be spent on public services is instead poured into the military. Hank Van Den Berg, Associate Professor of Economics at the University of Nebraska–Lincoln, estimated in The Nebraska Report, May/June 2011, that total annual military-related expenditures top $1.2 trillion and the interest on the federal debt spent on military activity is nearly $200 billion per year. That's taxpayer money that could be spent on education, job creation and a national health care program. Instead, it is going to service this debt and finance these wars, while school budgets are cut, jobs are outsourced to countries with lower wages, and Americans are made redundant with little or no safety net and no health insurance, while the directors of weapons manufacturers pocket the profits. The Roman Empire found it expensive to control Egypt for its grain.

The religious right are fond of quoting scripture, but here's one passage they tend to forget. "For the love of money is the root

---

[5] https://www.youtube.com/watch?v=Gg-jvHynP9Y

of all evil: which while some coveted after, they have erred from the faith, and pierced themselves through with many sorrows" (1 Timothy 6.10). Money has become the central pursuit of American life. Americans are bombarded with advertisements in their homes, on street signs, on passing buses, at toll booths, even in schools. There is a kind of frenzy of buying in American life.

Money has become more important than education. It's become so important that we're willing to charge students hundreds of thousands of dollars to get a university education, and we make them borrow that money at interest rates of between 6 and 8 percent. This is tying up disposable income in student loan repayment that could otherwise be reinvested in the economy through consumer spending. My student loan debt is $206,000. My monthly payment for my undergraduate debt was $695. Now that I have a PhD, once my loans come out of deferment, my monthly payment will be well over $1,000.

Many Americans are in the same straits. While wages began to stagnate in the early 1970s, cost of living has continued to rise. People make up the difference with credit. Americans have been paying with credit since at least the 1800s, but it really took off in the mid-1960s, after the first general use credit card—BankAmericard, which later became Visa— was franchised nationally. Debt began to skyrocket almost immediately. Average household debt was $27,600 in 1962 (adjusted for inflation), according to Federal Reserve Board data. In 2004, it was $79,100. One in three Americans is being pursued by a debt collector. That is up from one in seven about five years ago.

Money has become more important than nutrition. Study after study wrings its hands over the obesity epidemic. The main culprit is identified as fast food, and while it is true that Americans consume vast quantities of it, the studies omit one of the big reasons for this. As the cost of living has gone up while wages have stagnated and health insurance coverage has shrunk, Americans have to work more and more hours just to run in place financially. By the end of the day, they are exhausted, and a swing past the drive-through window of McDonald's is a much more tolerable option to going home and cooking. For poor Americans, McDonald's dollar menu is a less expensive way to feed a family than a meal cooked with healthy ingredients bought from a supermarket.

What most studies also don't say is that one of the reasons many Americans are overweight is that they are too poor to buy healthy food. A 2006-2007 study by the University of Washington's Center for Obesity Research found that a 2,000-calorie diet of high-energy, low-nutrition junk food costs $3.52 a day, while eating nutrient-rich foods such as fruits, vegetables and high-protein foods costs $36.32 a day. I grew up in a family on Food Stamps. We ate government cheese. We ate government peanut butter loaded with sugar. The only vegetables we ate were canned because we couldn't afford fresh, or even frozen. I did not eat a fresh vegetable until I was 16. It was broccoli, and I ate it raw with bleu cheese dressing alone on my first night in my own flat. It was, without exaggeration, life-changing.

It is also the case that there are often no grocery stores in poor neighborhoods, only corner stores where no healthy food can be bought. The poor often lack cars to drive to grocery stores, and it is incredibly difficult to carry bags of groceries home on the bus or subway, often with children in tow. Many poor people live in low-income hotels with unreliable ovens, so they couldn't cook the groceries even if they could get them home. Other research has shown that obesity, diabetes mortality and calorie consumption are associated with income inequality in developed countries, and that increased nutritional problems may be a consequence of the psychosocial impact of living in a more hierarchical society.

Money has become more important than health care. In 2010, some 52 million Americans lacked health insurance, up from 38 million in 2001. The Affordable Care Act—Obamacare—improved the situation to some extent—by 2016, 9 out of 10 Americans had health insurance under the Act,[6] meaning that now only 28 million Americans were uninsured—but the monthly premiums remain high. According to a study of ACA health plans, in 2020 the average national premium for an individual was $456 a month, while for a family it was $1,152.[7] That is $5,472 a year for an individual and $13,824 for a family. (This study did not take into account people with government subsidies). For people who still get health insurance through their employers, a study by the Kaiser Family Foundation found that in 2020 the average national premium for an individual was $622 a month, while for a family it was $1,778 a month.[8] That is $7,470 yearly for an individual and $21,342 yearly for a family. Coverage through employers still comes with high deductibles and other out-of-pocket costs for prescriptions, co-pays and other costs, while expansion of

---

[6]https://policyadvice.net/insurance/insights/affordable-care-act-statistics/
[7]https://www.ehealthinsurance.com/resources/individual-and-family/how-much-does-individual-health-insurance-cost
[8]https://www.kff.org/report-section/ehbs-2020-summary-of-findings/

coverage under the Affordable Care Act was achieved mostly through Medicaid expansion. This is good news for poor people, but it means that working-class and middle-class people receive much less support. Forty percent of the American population didn't receive any help at all. Access to healthcare under the ACA has also been spotty. People on Medicaid have suffered from narrow networks of providers, and those who got their coverage through exchanges or their employers face high out-of-pocket costs.[9] The main reason for this is that President Obama's original bill was largely gutted, the public insurance option having been eliminated thanks to Republicans getting the tie-breaking vote they needed to kill the public option from Joe Lieberman, a Democratic senator from Connecticut, home to so many of the insurance companies who would lose money under the bill. The loss of the public option meant that the private insurers didn't have to compete for customers and thus had less incentive to lower their prices, leaving nearly thirty million people still priced out. Under Donald Trump, Republicans made in-roads to further reducing coverage. The Trump administration cut outreach and education funding for the program by 90 percent in August 2017, and shortened the sign-up period, so even if people did know they are eligible for Obamacare, they may miss the chance to register for it. In September 2017, Congress let a program expire that provided healthcare for 9 million low-income children. President Biden has taken steps to strengthen Obamacare, but so far in 2022 nearly 30 million Americans still have no health insurance. That is not his fault, and it is not Obama's. It is the fault of conservative voters and the politicians they continue to return to office, who still value money over health.

---

[9] https://pubmed.ncbi.nlm.nih.gov/28339427/

It is the result of something deep within us. Americans do not want to think they can't take care of their families. It is easier to believe that if somebody is poor it's their own fault than to admit that the American Dream is not working. Americans do not like bad news. As for their own struggles, there is always a president, a city council, an immigrant to blame.

This belief that the poor and other people who are suffering must have done something to cause it is an attitude that *Divine Magnetic Lands* author Timothy O'Grady noticed when he moved to Ireland in 1973. "I found something else that I'd seen little of in America," he said, "the idea that chaos and helplessness are never far away from anyone, that they just take you as a strong wind takes a tree, and that their victims are to be commiserated with rather than scorned."

The American swing to the right coincided with a precipitous drop in union membership and the beginning of the stagnation of wages in 1973. Perhaps this is when working people began seeing themselves in common cause with the elite. Whereas working-class Americans used to see themselves as persecuted by the rich, they began to think of themselves as a different interest group—the morally upright—and imagined their values under attack by liberals and their immoral ideas. They severed their union ties, and the freefall began.

Many people are also still laboring under the delusion that if you work hard, you will become rich. This is for the most part untrue, but they believe it. Perhaps they don't want to raise taxes on the rich because they think that one day they might be rich and will have to pay those taxes themselves. But more than that, I think, they want to identify with the rich, or rather, they want the rich to identify with them. We idolize wealth in America; it is our national pastime and our religion. Wealth is good, so under our ideology, the wealthy are good. We want them to like us, to accept us, because we want to be like them.

We are also more punitive than other developed countries. The prison and jail population in the United States has skyrocketed from about 380,000 people in 1975 to 2.2 million in 2007, according to Jason DeParle, 'The American Prison Nightmare.' As of 2007, DeParle writes, seven Americans in every 1,000 were behind bars. That is about five times the historic norm and seven times higher than most of Western Europe. And while Black people make up 13 percent of the U.S. population, they account for 38 percent of the people incarcerated.

Money is more important than life. After twenty children and six staff were shot to death at Sandy Hook Elementary School, my friends said: Now we will have gun control. I knew we wouldn't. The power of the gun lobby would prevent it. So it proved to be. Congress valued the campaign contributions of the NRA more than the lives of six- and seven-year-old children.

I moved to Savannah, Ga., on the last day of 2001, still looking for America. I had warm memories of the South from childhood, visiting our people during summers in Virginia, days running with cousins through the grass in their vast back yard, everyone brown and dopey from the sun, catching fireflies at dusk. I found some of America there. Southerners were gregarious and interested in you and what you were doing, and charitable to a fault when a neighbor had a crisis. I saw flyers tacked up in Waffle House for fish fries and Poker Run fundraisers for locals in need—a toddler who needed a heart transplant, a woman battling cancer. I had to walk home from work one night because I had a flat tire and no auto club insurance. When I got to work the next morning, the mayor was kneeling before my car changing the tire. As he worked and we chatted, the mayor pro tem drove by, saw us, pulled up and got out to help. I heard about a woman who used to have a pet alligator but he got out of the car at church.

But I also met people who cheered the war in Afghanistan, and then in Iraq, even though their young sons and husbands were deploying in disproportionate numbers. I met a man who tried to preach to me. I told him I was agnostic. He asked me, "If you don't believe in God, how do you keep from killing people?" I saw Confederate battle flags displayed in the windows of pickup trucks, often above a rifle or shotgun. I saw a bumper sticker that said: 'Union 1, Confederacy 0. Halftime.' I watched Sen. Max Cleland, a Vietnam veteran who lost both legs and an arm in the war, lose his re-election bid to Republican Saxby Chambliss. When I met Cleland for an interview just before the election, I watched his aides lift him from his unassuming Honda into a wheelchair, and I offered my left hand because he had no right hand to shake. Cleland lost the election a week later after Chambliss ran TV ads calling him a traitor for his Senate votes against homeland security legislation. And I saw a people who, collectively, in their politics, were shockingly unwilling to help thy neighbor.

Those people elected Donald Trump, who put children in cages, who eroded any sense of decency both in American politics and in daily life, who encouraged racists and xenophobes and homophobes and transphobes and every other hateful person to give vent to their very worst instincts, who summoned a mob to overthrow the government and brought us to the brink of dictatorship.

The rest of the world, too, will now view us differently. Even should we undo all the things Trump has done, even with the election of Joe Biden in 2020, the world will not easily forget what we have done. They will look at us and think: You did it once. You might do it again. And they will be right.

So how do we fix it all? Maybe the answer is we don't. Maybe it's time to call it a day, to admit that we are ungovernable as we are presently constituted. We are so polarized that nobody gets the government they want, and we are appalled by each other. The conservatives have pulled the Democratic Party ever farther to the right, and the best we have managed to do is to fend off some of the very worst instincts of the Republican Party, protect Roe v. Wade—as of this writing, at least, though perhaps not for long—and keep them from tipping us over into authoritarianism. Now Roe is under threat of being overturned, and we still stand at the precipice of dictatorship if Trump is re-elected or someone like him or worse comes along. While people stand in lines at food banks, meat packers are forced to go to work while COVID-19 rages through the facility, and people are having their water shut off in a pandemic because they can't pay the bill. The people who voted for Donald Trump and Republicans like him are destroying my America, the one we're supposed to be, the one we claim we are. They've been doing it for decades.

It's difficult to make the leap of imagination necessary to think of the United States breaking up. We have internalized the ideas of Manifest Destiny and the shining city on the hill. But we are still relatively young as nations go. It would not be surprising that the original blueprint needed adjusting as we matured and developed a better idea of who we are and who we want to be. We take for granted that we are immune from the schisms that have rent other countries into new and separate nations. A democracy needs constant renewal if it is to survive. We have not done the work necessary to ensure that we were endeavoring to be who we set out to be. For a long time, we haven't even tried. We need to think creatively about ourselves, interrogate our ambitions as a people, forget about who we are and focus on who we want to be, and maybe we decide that what 56 percent of us want to be is fatally incompatible with what the other 44 percent want. I do not say this easily. My heart hurts at the thought.

Older people for whom America worked will be shocked at this suggestion. For them, America is not just an idea. They did do a little better than their parents. They bought tidy little houses. They remember the heady days of World War II when we fought Nazism and fascism, and the jet-fueled economy created by the need for military hardware that created a prosperity that lasted well into the 1960s. For some people. Many of them were able to send their children to college. But many of those children have not done as well. I am one of them, and still, a few years ago, I would not have even considered such a thing. But things have gotten worse. So much worse. That is to say, our worst selves have broken into the open so violently, and seized the levers of government in a way that seemed unimaginable before, that I can no longer pretend it is not who many of us are.

I have a friend, a community organizer, who refers to America as a slaver's republic. She says that nothing can be done to save it. Let it die and salt the earth is her message. This used to anger me. It still does. Perhaps it frightens me, this idea that my country is nothing more than its slaving past, that the better angels of our nature do not exist as Lincoln told us they did, that the invention of public schools, the great melting pot, and the moon landing meant nothing, that everything else has always been a lie.

This anger may simply be instinctive, my automated response to criticism of my country, a phantom pain in a dead limb. That's the part of me that can't help loving my country. There is much that I love about America. A leisurely walk up Fifth Avenue towards the Met sets my heart racing, anticipating the beauty of the art and artefacts I will see in the museum and the people-watching I will enjoy in Central Park afterwards. A gentle breeze rustling Spanish moss amidst a canopy of live oaks in Savannah makes my heart ache with the beauty of it. The music—Billie Holiday, Sonny Rollins, Champion Jack Dupree, Louis Prima, Bob Dylan—feels like the sins and joys of our people laid bare. We are boisterous and enthusiastic and, until recently, almost boundlessly optimistic.

And despite what my friend says, I maintain that we have achieved great things, that we are more than a slaver's republic. That a majority of us want desperately to live up to the idea of America. That is why I say that we no longer work as we are presently constituted, and that it's time to think fresh, to imagine ourselves anew.

Because make no mistake, we *have* been a slaver's republic, and those sentiments and that hatred has bubbled beneath the surface ever since, until Trump coaxed it all into the open, emboldened those who held those ideas. But he did not create them. Indeed, he is the result of them. They are in our bones. In a network news segment on the white supremacist and neo-Nazi attacks in Charlottesville, two African American commentators, both Republicans, fought through tears to speak. White people can never fully comprehend the pain people of color feel because we are not subjected to the marginalization, disenfranchisement, hostility, and overt violence people of color have to endure daily, hourly, minute by minute.

But if we want to really change we must, finally, acknowledge it. This is not a conservative problem; it is an American problem. It is not a modern problem; it is a foundational problem. Until we bow to it, grow humble before it, and figure out how to stop it, we will never be the America we claim to be. I can't see 44 percent of us being willing to do that work.

After Charlottesville and the sight of neo-Nazis marching on American streets, a British friend told me, "Let us do whatever it is we do when prayer seems called for." I am not religious, and so I find myself not knowing what to do. I call my senators and congressman, I sign petitions, I vote, I write. None of it changes anything. I do not know what to do next. I do not know what can be done. The ideas on which America was founded have never been fully realized, but there were times when we were on our way. Now, it seems as though we've strayed so far from the path, I don't see how we can find our way back.

So maybe we should consummate the split that we thought had been repaired after The Civil War. Let them go. It is hard to remember now why Lincoln's dream of an America stretching from one coast to the other was important when cancer patients are left to die for lack of healthcare and people in Tennessee line up once a year outside tents to have their rotting teeth pulled by dentists out of charity. Where a black child is shot for buying Skittles and his murderer signs autographs at gun shows. Where we put children in cages. Let those people in their new nation call themselves the Confederate States of America, or whatever they like. The rest of us can be a nation of the East and West coasts and a strip of land connecting us along the northern border so the trucks can ship goods back and forth. If North Dakota, Montana and Idaho don't want to join us, I'm sure Canada will be happy to give us a strip of land along their southern border so that we can be contiguous and so that they will no longer share a border with a country that could become a fascist state at any moment. Maybe we would eventually divide even further into the eleven countries Colin Woodard has identified[10] or something like them.

When I look at his map and the regions into which he's divided us, with Yankeedom inheriting its ideas of morality from the abolitionists of its history, I can see one way forward for us. There is evil everywhere, but with luck—and work, and a commitment to decency—those who espouse it would be vastly outnumbered and would once again occupy the lunatic fringe they were until lately considered to occupy in America.

We must not delude ourselves that our shortcomings are merely a Southern problem. They are not. George Floyd was

---

[10] https://www.washingtonpost.com/gdpr-consent/?next_url=https%3a%2f%2fwww.washingtonpost.com%2fentertainment%2fbooks%2famerican-nations-by-colin-woodard-a-study-of-our-rival-regional-cultures%2f2011%2f10%2f10%2fgIQAvl1IZN_story.html

killed in Minneapolis, Michael Brown in Missouri, Amadou Diallo in New York City. Some Italian Americans in the Northeast still refer to African Americans as *moulinyan*. Somebody I knew growing up, when he felt he was being ignored or mistreated, used to say "What am I, colored?" But we cannot begin the work of striving towards decency when we are debating the morality of forced sterilizations of migrant women or whether the seventeen-year-old who killed two people and injured a third at a protest over the shooting death of a black man by a police officer was a good person.

We must recover our humanity. Once we have done that, only once we have done that, can we begin to do the work of self-examination that is necessary to appeal to the better angels of our nature that Lincoln talked about. Forty-four percent of us don't believe that work is necessary. This is not a bridgeable gap. So it's best we part company.

Tell me I'm wrong. March in the streets and demand a return to decency. The 46.8 percent who voted for Donald Trump in the 2020 election, 74,222,958 of you, stand up and say you were wrong, you repent, *Mea culpa, mea culpa, mea maxima culpa.* Please. I beg you.

When I think of America now, I feel something like the *hiraeth* I feel when thinking of where I grew up. But I've stopped looking for my America. The thought of that breaks my heart, but then again, I'm American. My heart was broken long ago.

MEN WHO LEAVE

I awake at three o'clock in the morning and realize that Deacon has not come to bed yet. I am in his apartment, a dingy little one-bedroom flat in Bayonne, New Jersey, which he rents from a Polish woman whose husband has died and whose children have all moved out on their own. She occupies the top floor, Deacon the bottom. I lie in bed staring at the stucco ceiling. The wall is bare but for a calendar and a few favorite photos affixed to the plaster with thumbtacks. The dresser is piled high with whatever scraps he has accumulated during the day, little bits of crumpled paper, articles he has ripped out of magazines at doctors' offices, loose change, E-Z Pass receipts. The place reeks of cigarettes, and the walls are a dingy yellow from the cloud of smoke that perpetually hangs in the air.

I am the child and grandchild of smokers. I struggled for fresh air my entire childhood. I was endlessly opening doors and windows in houses to get a cross breeze, rolling down car windows to hang my head out, sitting outside listening to the conversation through the screen door while the adults inside smoked and laughed. Whenever I am in Deacon's apartment, I taste nicotine on my tongue and feel smoke in my lungs, but I keep coming over. After a while I fling back the covers and get out of bed and go in search of my erstwhile lover.

This is the way it always is. I come over, we watch television for a while, Deacon treats me to his extended analyses of the political and philosophical implications of whatever we watched (which were admittedly brilliant because Deacon was a genius, but honestly, how long does anyone want to talk about Newt Gingrich?), then I would run out of steam and announce I was going to sleep. He would kiss me goodnight, and I would go into his room to sleep, leaving him to play video games on his computer or argue with the right wingers who ran the Web site he loved to hate, FreeRepublic.com. Deacon was a rabid leftist and delighted in taunting his counterparts on the right. It was his whole life. He would log on at work, at home, anywhere he had time. He had several screen identities. Sometimes he would pose as one of their own—Freepers, they called themselves—and express nagging doubts about some conservative ideal or another that they were espousing. Other times he would log on under the screen name left-wing angel and taunt them openly.

I am a liberal myself, but I could not understand why he was willing to give up so much of his time arguing with people who he was not going to convince of anything. Leave them be, I would tell him. You're never going to change their minds. But he never gave up. Whenever he entered a post, he could not wait to get back to the computer and see what the Freepers had to say about it. Eventually, usually about four a.m., he would come to bed, wake me for sex, and then go to sleep. I would wake up in the morning, we'd have sex again, then he'd go back to sleep and I'd sit outside and read until Deacon woke up. On weekends he would sleep well into the afternoon.

I emerged from the bedroom. Sure enough, there was Deacon, at the computer, banging away furiously at the keyboard, locked in mortal political combat with the Freepers. The apartment was strewn with crap, papers and clothes, some clean, some dirty, and empty plastic grocery bags, and whatever else Deacon had that he didn't care to put away, which was most everything he owned. In the kitchen sat a blue plastic picnic cooler filled with frozen dinners floating in tepid water. He had been using it as a freezer ever since his refrigerator broke a month ago. He still hadn't gotten around to telling the landlady that it needed to be replaced. He stopped at the gas station near the house on his way home every night for fresh bags of ice to fill it with.

"Hey, babe," he said when he saw me out of the corner of his eye. "I'm just about to come to bed, I just want to finish this post."

I went to him and encircled his chest with my arms and watched over his shoulder for a minute as he typed. I loved his chest. He was a large man, six-foot-two and broad-shouldered. He had a big belly, but I didn't care. I loved wrapping my arms around him and feeling the hardness of his chest, the maleness of it, the nest of black hair in the center. Seeing he wasn't anywhere near finished, I went back to bed.

Awhile later, I awoke to the sounds that told me Deacon was preparing to come to bed. His computer went to sleep, and Deacon began the ritual shuffling he went through every night before bedtime. This included several trips between the kitchen and the living room. Both rooms lay in view of the bedroom, and I watched as he passed back and forth before the open doorway, each time stepping on what I had noticed earlier was a notification from the DMV that his car registration was about to expire. I had pointed it out to him, but he just said, "Mmm hmm," and went back to the Freepers. I knew better than to move the paper, as this would disrupt his entire world, so I just left it there.

He passed over the paper again, leaving it in his path between the living room and the kitchen, on the theory that if he picked it up, he would only lose it, whereas if he left it where it was, it would serve as a constant reminder every time he stepped over it, until he finally picked it up and did something about it.

209

The only trouble was that he did the same thing with most important papers, so that new important ones just piled up on top of old important ones exactly where they fell, and he never thought any more about them until his annual cleaning. Then he would come across these papers, be visited with the momentary panic that he had not done anything about them, then realize it was too late now anyway, shrug, and toss them in one of the green garbage bags he would later drag out to the curb.

No two ways about it. Deacon was depressed.

He was on medication now, which helped considerably but still could have benefited from adjustment. He didn't have the ambition, however, to do much about it, still not convinced that there was anything wrong with him other than the fact that he was a whiner. It had taken six months and all of my energy to convince him to seek medication in the first place, and I was not up to another prolonged campaign just now. Instead, I watched him self-medicate with the marijuana pipe he took hits from all day long. It did not go unnoticed by me that I was attempting to convince a lover to seek mental health treatment in the same way that I for years attempted to convince my mother to take her bipolar medication, have her dose adjusted, change her medication. Rather than understand that I was replicating that relationship and end it, I stayed and kept trying. This is part of the shame growing up poor can grind into you. *No one normal will want you. You'll have to make do with this.* And also, *you can fix it. I know you couldn't fix her, but if you try hard enough, you can fix him.*

Deacon was 20 years older than me. I almost invariably date older men. Everybody tells me this is because I am looking for a father figure. I usually point out that my mother, in fact, had been the more damaging parental figure in my life—well, that's not true; more like the more chaotic and more absent, and therefore presumably the one whose love and approval I would most seek to achieve by proxy in a relationship. That did nothing to change peoples' convictions, partly because most people tend not to want to criticize mothers and partly because having arrived at what to them was a serviceable diagnosis of my problem, they were loath to rethink it.

I once read a psychological study that found that, contrary to previous theories, everybody—men and women alike—actually sought out their *mother* to duplicate in relationships, but I did not share this information with the armchair therapists in my life. It would not convince them, and furthermore, I had recently discovered a pattern in my choice of men that fit this theory. I seemed exclusively to choose men I could not trust. Not necessarily that they would deceive me, though they often did, but rather that I could not depend on them emotionally, and that seemed to me to be just like my mother. This, however, wasn't anybody's business but my own, and I kept it to myself, as I did most everything else.

One of the first things he told me when we started dating was that he didn't want kids. He had avoided having them when he was younger because his father had died at age 30 and he thought he would do the same and leave his children fatherless. But he didn't.

"I could've raised the bastards by now," he said.

I already knew I didn't want kids. I worried I would be a selfish parent like my mother or be rageful like my father. So Deacon not wanting them either was just fine with me.

I have never been physically abused in a relationship. For whatever reason, in spite of all the emotional abuse I did allow, I never allowed that. One boyfriend tried. As is usually the case with such things, the mistreatment escalated. Early in our relationship, he threw a drink in my face. I tried to be the bigger person and walked away. Another time he called me a worthless welfare cunt. That time I slapped him hard across the face, so I suppose from this perspective you could say that it was I who introduced physical violence into the relationship. The first time he tried to physically abuse me, he shoved me hard, and my experience in the projects kicked in. Without thinking I used what I remembered of my karate training to deliver a side kick to his stomach. A long time passed, many months, I think, then he tried once more, and I delivered a roundhouse kick to his face and knocked him flat on his back. He never tried to hit me again. We stayed together another year before I finally broke up with him. I don't even remember why.

Eventually Deacon came to bed and we made love. Whatever was not working in our relationship, sex was not it. From the very beginning, the sex between us came naturally and was extraordinary. Tonight was no exception, and afterward we lay peacefully intertwined.

"I do like lying around the house with you," he said. "Or anywhere, for that matter. And not just lying around in bed, come to think of it."

This is as far as he would go, I knew, and so I did not try to push him farther, though I didn't change the subject, either. I may have surrendered the upper hand in this relationship—I was aware that I had violated the cardinal rule where men are concerned: Don't ever let them know they've got you. It inspires in all men an uncontrollable flight reflex, or at least it does in the men I've chosen and in the world I grew up in, but I wasn't going to be *that* easy. I just lay there next to him and let his remark hover in the air between us, with all its implied affection, and let him decide whether to expound upon it or counter it. I knew he would choose to counter it, probably by opening up a wide expanse of mattress between us that night until he thought I'd fallen asleep, at which point he would wrap himself around me and kiss me gently on the forehead, thinking I didn't feel it.

Sure enough, he pulled away from me, went to the easy chair by his bedroom window and lit a cigarette. He pulled up the shade and looked out over the dim street lit only by a far-off streetlamp, the appropriate distance between us now established. I would have to wait now until he thought I was asleep before any further affection would be proffered. Another such time when he'd been on the receiving end of some especially satisfying fellatio, shivering as he climaxed, he drew me to him afterward, obviously thrown off guard.

"I may be a man past his prime, but I tell you what, I'm having the best sex of my life." Quick to correct the damage of this intimacy, he offered a quick quip. "I guess it's because I don't have to do all the work."

I lay there wondering why I didn't get out of the bed, get dressed and storm out, possibly hitting him with something heavy on the way. Instead, I let only silence demonstrate my hurt feelings. It registered with him, as I knew it would, or he may have even concluded all on his own without my feeble silent protest that he had gone too far. The following weekend, when we lay in bed afterward, he stroked my back softly while he caught his breath.

"I tell you what," he said, "I'm having the best sex of my life. That has to have something to do with you."

"So am I," I said.

Returning the compliment, but still safe. I wasn't giving away too much power, but I was also leaving the door open for him to walk through if he ever finally chose to do so. It also had the benefit of being true, which allowed me the safety of not having merely said it out of love.

"Well, shit," he said.

"You smell good," I said, the best substitute I could think of for what I wanted to say.

"So do you," he said. "The coincidences keep popping up."

That is as far as he would go, and the only thing that kept him from withdrawing is that I didn't try to push the conversation to its logical next step. Instead, I lay there wondering how it had come to pass that I pretended this was enough for me.

I do not want to write this. It is humiliating and demeaning and demoralizing. It shows me at my worst, shows some of the worst choices I have ever made, the worst things I have ever done, and when I read it back I cringe. How could you have allowed someone to treat you this way? I think. And how could you have done this? Growing up as I did, I had learned quickly to defend myself against physical attack, sexual attack, mental attack, verbal attack. It has left its scars, god knows it has, but I learned. However, the subtle, meticulous process through which the men I have chosen in my life wore me down, belittled me, made me feel unworthy of their love, made me feel grateful for the scraps of affection and time they tossed at me, *that* I was not prepared for. And that is what got me. That is why I am writing this. To understand how the shame of growing up poor impacts on every relationship in your life, you will have to hear—I will have to tell you—how it affected my relationships with men, guided the men I chose, and ensured that those men were always men who would refuse to love me, were always men who leave.

I am calling this particular man Deacon, though that was not his name, because at this period in his life he had got religion. In my experience two types of people almost invariably get religion at one time or another: prisoners and recovering addicts. Deacon was a recovering alcoholic, and his sponsor got him reading the Bible, and by the time I met him he was a committed Baptist, and a radical one. He had developed all kinds of theories about the end times, the specialness of Jews, and why they excelled at every profession they turned their hands to.

"Have you heard his theory about God?" his friend Trey once asked me.

"What theory about God?"

"That he's real?"

Deacon and Trey grew up together in Arkansas, and I met Deacon when he moved to New York City to try to become an actor. I once mentioned this to a friend who asked me about the new man I was dating.

"He's from Arkansas?"

"Yeah."

"Jesus."

While he was still living in Arkansas, and still drinking, Deacon once spent the day drinking Lone Star beer after a fight with his girlfriend, and then went to a party that night, picked up the phone the minute he walked in the door, and called her.

"He stood there screaming at her for two hours," Trey told me years afterwards. "I saw her later and I asked her, 'how could you listen to him for that long?' And she said, 'Are you kidding me? I hung up after two minutes.'"

Deacon was so drunk he didn't even realize he was screaming down an empty phone line for two hours. Once he realized his girlfriend was no longer on the phone, he hung up and climbed out the homeowner's bedroom window and attempted to jump into the adjacent tree. He jumped, grabbing for a branch, but missed and fell two stories to the ground and broke his arm.

The next day he went to his first AA meeting.

One other thing: Deacon was married. His wife lived back home in Arkansas, and they saw each other two weeks a year, she visiting him in New York one week and he visiting her in Arkansas the other. This is how I rationalized dating a married man. If a man saw his wife two weeks out of the year, was he really even married? In a way he seemed more married to me than her. He discussed important decisions with me. Should I buy a new car? He brought me with him to furniture stores to pick out a new couch. He asked which one I liked, and should we get a chair to go with it? He called on Thursday nights to say he was going to the grocery store and what foods did I want for the weekend. We even went on double dates with his friend Trey and his wife. We went to their house for dinner. If it was warm out, we played bridge afterwards on their sleeping porch.

Deacon and I dated, if you could call it that, for about three years. In ways he could be incredibly caring. After 9/11, he insisted on me leaving the city (I was living in Brooklyn at the time) and coming to stay with him in New Jersey where, he said, it would be safer. This seemed like a reasonable suggestion, and I also wanted to see him and thought that the idea that he wanted me safe—and that safe meant being with him—meant something, that somehow 9/11 had changed things between us. His normal work commute involved taking the PATH train from Jersey City and transferring to the subway beneath the Towers, and I worked two blocks away and my subway tracks travelled beneath the Towers, and both of us were late for work that morning and missed our respective trains. Those circumstances kept us away from the Towers at 8:46 that morning, and in those twin coincidences, I thought perhaps he saw some message. So, I said I would pack a bag and grab the next train. But he worried that the attacks were not over yet and that my train might be bombed and instead insisted on driving in to get me. In order to do this, he had to sit in traffic for five hours waiting for every car before him to go through the security checks that had been implemented on the inbound side of the George Washington Bridge into the city. He drove me to the donation drop-off point in Jersey City to deliver socks to the rescue workers, we went on drives in the Pine Barrens and along the shoreline. These may seem like small things that should be expected of a partner, but getting Deacon to leave his computer screen for more than a few hours was usually a trial so this felt like the Earth had shifted on its axis.

Most of the time, though, he was as I have described. Refusing to call me his girlfriend, even though we spent every single weekend together for three years, constantly saying we should stop seeing each other, that he was too old for me, that I was too young for him, that he didn't feel 'butterflies.'

And yet we kept on.

It only ended because I took custody of my baby sister and, wanting to get her away from the unhealthy environment in which she was living, moved with her to Savannah, Georgia. Two months after I left, Deacon quit New York and moved back to Arkansas.

"New York doesn't feel like New York anymore without you," he said.

Then why the hell don't you marry me? I thought. But I said nothing.

He divorced his wife immediately after returning to Arkansas.

About six months after I moved, Deacon called asking if he could come visit. I still missed him desperately at this point, so I said yes.

"One thing," he said. "Will sex be on the menu? I don't mean to be crass, but it's a long drive."

Unbelievably, I said yes.

He stayed for a week, and it was like old times, which is to say, it was both wonderful and heartbreaking.

At the end of his visit, as he drove up the dirt drive and onto the paved road and out of sight, I had a strange feeling. I felt like I would never see him again. He called me a week later and told me he'd passed out and been taken to the hospital, and when he woke up they told him he had stage 4 adenocarcinoma and had six months to live.

He began chemo. He started to lose weight and had to stop working, and the government put him on Medicare, which means they must have been convinced he would die soon because he was only 55. But his body seemed to fight back, and the tumor shrank in size. He was weaker than he had been, but he felt all right.

"Can I come visit?" he said over the phone. "I want to see you while I still outweigh you."

He drove from Arkansas to Georgia, and because he had always wanted to see the Keys, we drove south to Florida. We had to stop and rest a lot because he was weak, so we didn't make it to the Keys, but we saw manatees swimming in a creek and we went to the Epcot World Showcase because he had never travelled much except when he was in the Navy during the Vietnam War and reckoned that at this point this would be the only way he would get to any of these countries. We ate troll horn in the Norway pavilion and crépes in the France pavilion and pizza in the Italy pavilion and bratwurst in the Germany pavilion. We then tried a few rides in Epcot, but Deacon began to feel unwell, so we went back to the motel, and the next morning we decided to turn around and head back.

Driving north on I-95 somewhere north of Jacksonville, a car cut in front of me and I hit the brakes. Nothing happened. The car continued at 65 miles per hour and the pedal went all the way to the floor. Luckily the car that had cut us off immediately accelerated so we didn't hit it. I saw a green exit sign so I slowed the car down and aimed for it. I pulled onto the exit. It was a long winding exit ramp that continued straight for about 100 feet before it bore right and then, I could see, would spill its traffic onto the frontage road below. Deacon talked to me quietly and gently.

"Okay, just let the car slow down until you get to the curve, then as soon as you make it all the way around and we're going straight again, steer the car onto the grass verge and hold tight to the steering wheel. We'll be okay."

I did as he told me to do. Just past the curve I eased the car right and onto the grassy verge, and it bumped and trundled and the steering wheel vibrated violently in my hands.

"Good. You're doing really well. Just hold her steady," Deacon said.

And what we hoped would happen happened. The bumps and dips in the grass slowed the car's momentum, and eventually it came to a stop just shy of the intersection with the frontage road. I let go of the steering wheel and exhaled slowly. Deacon stroked my hair.

"That was excellent. You did a great job. I can't believe how calm you were."

We called AAA and they towed the car to a garage and dropped us off at a Ramada Inn. We watched TV and lounged around and ate in the hotel restaurant for two days while the mechanics fixed the car.

It felt like a metaphor for our entire relationship. Always careening along towards an uncertain conclusion, all the time with me in the driver's seat, in the best position to control the outcome, yet allowing Deacon to dictate what happened.

I saw Deacon one more time after that. He had just been dumped by a woman he'd been in love with since he was in his twenties. He had called me a few months earlier, when they'd started dating again, said he felt he owed it to me. They hadn't seen each other in fifteen years and he bumped into her at a party, and they started in again, as though no time had passed at all.

"She just feels like my soul mate," he said. "I feel like I want to bond with her. I always did."

I ignored the cruelty of this remark, and the fact that he didn't seem to recognize it was cruel, and I wished him well. A few weeks later, I came home from work to about 35 frantic messages on my answering machine from Deacon's mother asking me where Deacon was and please to have him call me and one from his friend Dash. I didn't even know how Deacon's mother got my number. I had never even met her. I guessed he must have given it to her. Before I could even get out of my coat, the phone rang again. I saw on the caller ID that it was Dash, so I picked it up. He said that Deacon had gone missing, been gone for a few days now, and his mother was just going crazy, and was he with me.

"No," I said, "why would he be here?"

"Well, he's not here, so I just assumed he was with you."

I guess our relationship was not as secret as Deacon had tried to keep it. I had met Dash only once, after a play they were both in. We all went out to dinner afterwards and, even though Deacon had introduced me as a friend visiting from Georgia, Dash immediately began treating us like a couple. Even Dash saw what Deacon could not. We had kept in touch through emails and phone calls after that.

I told him that I had not seen Deacon since his last visit and that I had no idea where he was and could he please ask Deacon's mother to stop calling me because she has used up all the tape on my answering machine.

Deacon called a few days later and apologized for his mama calling me so much. He and this new woman had gone to New Orleans and he didn't want anybody to know where he was (I don't know why), so he told his mother he was going to visit me. So not only had he dumped me for some woman who hadn't sought fit to commit to him thirty years ago, but he used me as his excuse, making me a target for his histrionic mother and her endless, increasingly unhinged phone calls. And that's only what he did to me, to say nothing of worrying his mother and his friends.

Anyway, he called one night a few weeks after that to tell me that the woman he'd left me for and run away to New Orleans with had dumped him again. He asked if he could come see me. I agreed, but I made it clear that this time there would be no sex and that he would be sleeping on the couch. I thought it was an opportunity for us to try to find a way to be friends.

He tried to get me into bed the day he arrived and kept trying, but I managed to resist, and he sulked and sighed the entire visit and made it really unpleasant and no fun at all. When he left we hugged coldly. I thought about it for a few days, and then I realized the way he had behaved during that visit was no different than the way he'd behaved the entire time I'd known him. The only difference was that all those other times he always got what he wanted. This time he hadn't. It was somewhere during this time that I became aware of the way my innate shame guided my choices in men and in the way I allowed those men to treat me. I decided that getting well meant eliminating from my life the people who made me feel like I didn't matter.

I emailed him and told him I could not see him anymore.

"Let's face it, we have never been any good for each other," I said. I wished him well and signed off. He called me every few months after that, increasingly frantic, but I never called him back. He's dying, I thought. He needs his friends. You should talk to him. But I simply could not bring myself to do it.

A few months later, Trey called to say that Deacon had died and that he had talked about me until the end. I have lived with the guilt ever since. I don't know if I did the right thing in cutting him off, but I know that sometimes a person is just finished. Next time would be different, I told myself. From now on, I would know my own worth, and I would not allow a man to make me feel that I did not have value.

And then I met Noble. Our first encounter was in the foyer of the newsroom I worked for at my first journalism job in Georgia. He had come to drop off a press release for something or other, and he asked for me specifically because the issue the press release concerned was part of my beat. (He confessed later that he had asked for me because he had seen me at a City Council meeting and was instantly smitten and vowed to find a way to meet me). He was very tall, well over six feet, and very handsome, which normally doesn't matter to me, but something about him made my heart hammer. I realized later that I recognized something in him, something self-destructive that I was going to seek to heal and something malignant that was going to seek to break me, but at the time I thought I simply found him attractive. He was educated, articulate, well-mannered, which is to say, not like the boys I had known in the projects, and not like the men who lived in the ghetto where my mother, brother and one sister still lived.

He was friends with a source I knew well, so when he said he'd just dropped his car off at the auto mechanic next door to be repaired and asked me in the most elegant Southern drawl I had ever heard if I could possibly give him a ride home, I gladly obliged. One of the perks of being a newspaper reporter is that you have a great deal of freedom in your personal movement. I told my editor that the man was a source and we were going to sit down at a restaurant for an interview, and left.

This was in the country outside Savannah, and Noble lived deep within it, way back in the woods beyond the Ogeechee River. It was May and the air conditioning in my car was broken, so I rolled down all the windows and we sailed along, first on pavement and then on ash roads, the wind whipping my hair all round my head, and I removed my hand from the steering wheel every few seconds to brush it from my face. I could feel Noble watching me, and I knew what he was thinking. *Don't care if her hair gets mussed. Don't wear makeup. Wild child.* Genteel Southerners enjoy using poor grammar ironically.

By the time we pulled into his driveway I was smitten.

"I thank you kindly for the ride," he said. "Would you like to come in for a few minutes? Have a glass of lemonade? I could show you the property. There are five acres back behind the house, and I've got corn growing and tomatoes. ('Tamatas,' he said.) And the pecan trees are ripe. They're dropping all over the yard."

He was bringing to bear every drop of Southern charm he had at his disposal. No one had ever warned me about charming men, and I was enthralled. And yet I would learn later that this charm, this drawl, this overacted gentility, was part of the story he told about himself, part of how he constructed his own identity, to himself as much as to everybody else. Without that, he would, as he told me one night, years later while drunk, be jolted awake every night to find himself alone, swimming in his own sweat, seized with spasms he realized were his own sobbing, cutting him to his knees on the cold floor, clawing at the air, begging, Oh God, please, begging for you don't even know what, just for it all to be over. Please, God. Oh, God, please. But that knowledge would come to me later.

I could have gone into Noble's house that afternoon. It had only been a half-hour drive, and my editor would not care if I didn't come back to the newsroom at all that day. He would simply assume I was chasing a story. But I remembered past mistakes, making myself too available to men I wanted, remembered Deacon, and I declined.

"I have to get back to work," I said. "Another time."

"Yes, ma'am," he said, by which he meant, *you won't get away from me that easy.*

He climbed out and closed the door and tapped on the window frame by way of goodbye, tapped with his left hand, and I saw his wedding ring.

A few days later he called to ask me to lunch on the pretext of discussing the article I'd written on the subject of the press release. That would be all right, I told myself. It's only lunch. We're not doing anything wrong. He wasn't a source or a news subject. We met at a barbecue joint near my newsroom. The waitress brought sweet tea and a basket of cornbread, and we talked for two hours, not a word of it about my article. He asked me many questions about myself, about where I grew up and what it was like living in New York and why I had moved to the South. He said how different I was from the people around here, so smart, so open-minded, and he let his hand brush mine for the briefest of moments, as though it were an accident, then reached for the napkin nearby and brought it to his lips.

It meant nothing, I told myself. He was just reaching for his napkin.

After lunch he asked if I would like to go for a drive. He wanted to show me something. I said yes and climbed into his Bronco, and we set off north on Route 21. A little ways outside of town he turned right, and we followed the road around to Old Ebenezer, the site of the county's original settlement by Salzburgers who had emigrated to the new colony of Georgia from what would later become Austria.

"They're still here," he said. "They're all over the county. Listen to the names. *Heidt. Rahn. Weissenbacher.*" He pronounced each name with precision, in an exaggerated German accent, and I connected the names with people I knew of in the county. We walked around and he showed me the exhibits and explained what they were all about and told me the history behind them. I had not had much of this kind of conversation since I left the city, and I marveled at his ability to contextualize the history he was sharing with me. History was and is of great fascination to me. It helps us understand who we are by helping us understand who our people were. Here was a man who shared this understanding and could show me new things.

Here was a man who came from money who didn't see that I was poor white trash.

We got back in the car and drove northwest to Old Louisville Road. Noble was fascinated with the road and its history, and we drove along it for miles, him pointing out sites and points of interest along the way. Eventually he leaned forward over the steering wheel and peered up at the pinking sky.

"We done drove the whole day away," he said. "I better get you home."

We drove back and he dropped me at my car outside the barbecue joint, and I was in love.

Unlike Deacon, who was Deacon from day one, a man I recognized as damaged and who admitted he was damaged and from whom I could have easily walked away had I not chosen to try to fix him, Noble hid himself for a long time. For many months, while he was courting me (grooming me might be a better way to say it), he was charming, kind, solicitous and complimentary.

He began calling me at night, first once or twice a week and then every night. I often wondered where his wife was during these calls, but it was also part of how I told myself we weren't doing anything wrong. If they were truly a couple in any way beyond staying married for the sake of appearances, his wife would not permit him to spend every night on the phone with me. I never heard any noise in the background, any shuffling or talk, any television or radio. Maybe she wasn't even home. Maybe she was out pursuing an illicit relationship of her own.

Noble enjoyed defying expectations, especially expectations of white Southern men. He spoke of the absolute justice of women's rights and civil rights.

"My mind is closed on certain subjects," he said. "On the subject of women's rights, my mind is closed. On the subject of civil rights, my mind is closed. Women and black folks have the same rights as everybody else. My mind is closed on those subjects, and I will not entertain other opinions."

I look back on that declaration now and see just how it was calculated to play to my liberal beliefs, to draw me in, but at the time I believed it utterly.

But he also enjoyed playing the old-timey Southerner, as though he had just stepped out of a sepia antebellum photograph in his white suit and straw boater hat, unfamiliar with the newfangled ways of the modern world. One evening the phone rang, and I saw his number on the caller ID, so I picked it up.

"Hey," I said.

Without returning the greeting he said, in that drawl that made my heart palpitate, "What is Pimp My Ride?" (It came out as "What is Pimp Ma Rahd?")

I called into the next room to my fifteen-year-old sister, who I knew would know.

"Charity! What's Pimp My Ride?"

And then I heard what sounded like hoofbeats as Charity tore in from the next room.

"Ooh!" she said, hands spread wildly, and began to describe in excited detail what the show and expression were all about.

When she was done, I said into the phone, "Did you get all that?"

"Well," Noble said, "I just don't know about all that stuff."

I found this unbelievably charming, just as he intended.

These nightly calls continued for months, the talk becoming more and more familiar, and with us staying on the phone later and later. Sometimes one of us fell asleep on the phone and one stayed on the line listening to the other breathe. We never spoke of what our relationship was growing into, but it was there. It sizzled in the air between us.

Now, Savannah is a town in which you cannot walk down the street without meeting someone you know. If you don't want to be seen in Savannah, don't go out. But I had an interview to do at the Metropolitan Planning Commission, so I drove down Route 21 into town, parked on Chatham Square near the Commission offices and headed over. I conducted my interview, and then it was lunchtime, so I walked over to a vegetarian lunch place I liked and got a wrap they made really well there, avocado with raisins and honey, lettuce and tomato and onions and a whole mess of other things. That night when I got home the phone rang. It was Noble.

"What was you doin down on Barnard Street in Savannah in the middle of the day when you sposed to be at your job?"

Noble enjoyed talking like he was just a simple country boy.

"You were in town?" I said. "Why didn't you come up and say hey?"

"I have not set foot in Savannah in two weeks."

"Then how do you know I was there today?"

"Shelby was sitting in Chatham Square eating his lunch and saw you walking by and called me on his cell phone and said, that girl you sweet on just walked right by."

Shelby was Noble's oldest and best friend.

I was caught off guard. This was the first time Noble had verbalized whatever it was that was between us. I didn't know what to say, and I stood dumb on the phone.

"So, what are we going to do?" he said suddenly.

"What are we going to do about what?" I said, though I knew what he meant.

He laughed, low and deep in this certain way he had. 'You're cute,' the laugh said, and also 'I see right through you.'

"I want to see you," he said. "I want to see all of you. I can't wait anymore."

And there it was, out in the open.

We decided he would come to my house on the following Tuesday at noon. My sister would be in school, and my landlord and landlady, who lived in the only house within sight of ours, were both reliably gone every Tuesday on business in South Carolina.

"I love you," he said as we lay in bed afterwards.

"I love you, too," I said.

After that, our affair began in earnest.

We spoke every night on the phone for hours, and when his wife went out of town on business, which was often, I stayed at his house. Arranging sleepovers for my sister at her friends' houses was easy, because she was at that age when she hated me and every other parental figure in her life and was happy to be away from home for extended periods, so I could stay at Noble's for days at a time.

The first night I stayed there, we slept in what he told me was the guest room, and I awoke feeling guilty about sleeping with a married man. This was different from Deacon. Deacon lived halfway across the country from his wife, but Noble and his wife lived under the same roof, and here I was in his bed. But I noticed as he went about getting dressed that all his clothes were in the closet and the dresser in that 'guest room,' and I soon understood that they slept in separate rooms. That is how I justified having an affair with another married man. If they slept in separate rooms, were they really even married?

We kept things very much concealed during the early days of our affair. We saw each other at night only at one another's houses. In the daytime we often went on drives in the country, and would sometimes go out to lunch, but that would be seen as perfectly harmless. Many people have lunch who are not sleeping together.

After a while, though, Noble began to bring us more out into the open, and he began to take reckless chances. One night we went for drinks at a bar in Savannah at which Noble was well known from years of socializing there in connection with his career. A woman across the bar knew him and looked me up and down and said, in a way that made it clear she knew I was not his wife, "Your wife is lovely, Noble."

Noble stroked my hair and let his arm rest around my shoulder.

"Oh, she's not my wife, but she is lovely."

I was nervous and asked him if he thought we ought to leave, but I was also giddy at the way he showed me around in the open, thinking it meant something. Thinking it meant he intended to leave his wife. To be with me.

We went dancing on Tybee, a little barrier island to the east of Savannah, and stayed in his family's beach house, a house that had been in his family for generations, and I thought this meant something, too. He was bringing me into the intimate spaces of his life. He was sharing his family's history with me, writing me into its story. Surely he was planning to leave his wife. That I would be breaking up a marriage by this time did not concern me. I wanted Noble. This man of privilege, who came from wealth, who lived on five acres of pecan trees and Georgia and loblolly pine and whose family owned a beach house, wanted me. I probably wanted him in part *because* he wanted me. I cared about nothing else.

Be wanted. Mold yourself in such a way that somebody will choose you.

This is of course self-defeating logic. Dating married men practically guarantees that they will not choose me, because they have already chosen someone else. And this is how I reproduce the relationship with my mother. I seek out someone in an effort to remake the past, the past in which my mother did not choose me; pick someone who will by definition not choose me, just as my mother did not; get my heart broken; repeat.

As the narcissist always does, he lured me in, charmed me, made me think I was the center of his world, and then once he had me, the psychological abuse began.

First his drinking got worse, or at least he let me see it more openly. Early on in our relationship he hid the extent of it, or I pretended I didn't notice it, or both. He always began drinking bourbon when I arrived at his house, and behaved as though he had just poured himself his first drink of the evening. For a while I let myself believe this. One morning as I rose from bed I walked past his study and saw him pick up the half-drunk glass of bourbon he had left there the night before and shoot back the dregs of whisky in the bottom of the glass. It was nine am. I chose to overlook it.

I was used to alcoholics. I was raised by them. In some way, they probably feel like home to me. He listened to Midnight Mass at his church one year on the radio from home because he was too drunk to make the drive into town. (His Episcopalian church, it should be noted, which in the United States is usually peopled by members of the moneyed class). He played a recording of it for me the next time I visited. He closed his eyes and listened as the choir sang 'O Come All Ye Faithful,' described how Father Pat would enter in procession as the sounds of the pipe organ washed over the congregation. The choir sang the Sanctus and the Benedictus in Latin, then the parishioners grew quiet and listened as Father Pat told them to live soberly, righteously and godly in this present world, and they spoke along with him the words of the Creed, and Deacon recited along in his cottony south Georgia drawl.

"We believe in one God, the Father, the Almighty, maker of heaven and earth, of all that is seen and unseen..."

At the words 'and was made man' he crossed himself, then got up and refilled his whisky glass.

Soon he began trying to evangelize me, first as a Republican and then into religion. I am an agnostic—not an atheist, mind you, but an agnostic, because I am so committed to the idea that I don't believe in God because it cannot be proven that he exists, I am also committed to the idea that I don't believe in atheism because it cannot be proven that he does not. A Czech cab driver I knew in Scotland once said to me, "If there is God, I cannot follow him. He is bad manager." That seemed to me about the best explanation for why there cannot be a God. What mad deity would allow a world such as this?

Noble began his evangelism stealthily, first by telling me he used to be a Democrat himself and agreed with many of their principles. Social Security, Medicare, the Great Society. All great Democratic programs. But, he said then, the party went too far to the left.

"I didn't leave the Democratic Party," he told me, stealing the line from Ronald Reagan, "the Democratic Party left me."

I realized much later that he meant that the party started letting black folks have the same rights as white folks, but at the time it went completely over my head.

He patronized me.

"Wait until you grow up a little," he said. "You'll see the error of your ways and become a Republican."

I was 33 years old. I pointed out to him that Jimmy Carter, Georgia's favorite son and 78 years old at that time, was still a Democrat. Noble ignored my comment and took a drink. That is what he always did when he did not have a rebuttal for something I said. He ignored me and took a drink.

When he saw he wasn't making any progress, he began telling me I should be going to church. I thought maybe he reasoned that if he could get me into the church, they would brainwash me into becoming a Republican. I told him I was an agnostic, so he made it his mission to convince me that God was indeed real and that my soul was in great peril if I did not accept Him and start attending mass.

"You were born a Catholic," he said. "How can you reject your family's faith?"

Though he did not know it, he was already on losing ground here. The extent of my family's Catholicism was fish on Fridays and the occasional Christmas Eve ritual of Midnight Mass.

"My father is a Jew," I reminded him. "Which means I'm also a Jew. And I reject it all. I don't believe in any of it. These are stories we told ourselves to make sense of things we didn't understand, only some people never stopped telling them, even when science came along to explain things to us."

"What about things science can't explain?"

"Like what?"

"Like why some people get cancer and others don't."

"You're saying that God has a reason for giving some people cancer and sparing others?"

He didn't answer me and just took a drink.

Usually as he got drunker, he grew angrier at my refusal to creep to the foot of the cross, and one night when I rebutted another of his arguments, he slammed his whisky glass down on the table.

"Goddamit, I am tellin you, you better come to Jesus."

I laughed at him. *Come to Jesus?* He got up and stormed out of the room.

Another time when he was running on and on about the similarities between himself and Winston Churchill, a favorite topic of his although there were no similarities beyond the fact that they were both depressive alcoholics, I tried to distract him.

"Kiss me," I said.

He did, but then drew away.

"Your mouth is bigger than mine," he said. I have full lips while his were thin, but what he really meant was 'you talk too much.'

A couple of years into our relationship, I was working in the newsroom on a Sunday night because I had to get a story finished, and the newsroom phone rang. Thinking it might be important, I answered it. It was Noble.

"What you doin there at this hour on a Sunday?"

I explained I had a breaking story to finish. He wanted to begin our normal evening conversation, but I told him I couldn't, I had to work. He harangued me, so I agreed to talk for just a few minutes. I don't remember what we were talking about, but the discussion grew adversarial. He was no doubt trying to talk politics. I rebutted a point he'd made and suddenly he grew volcanic.

"Shut your mouth, bitch."

I was stunned. He had been condescending to me before, and had demeaned my opinions, but he had never spoken to me that way. I hung up. The newsroom phone rang and rang after that, but I refused to answer it. When he finally got me on the phone the next day he apologized, I don't remember the exact words. I don't know why I stayed with him after that. I told myself that wringing an apology from him was a victory, that I had stood up for myself and won.

I never once asked him to leave his wife. I do not know why. Maybe I knew he wouldn't. Even though he called her horrible names, 'boar hog' and 'witch' and 'swamp trash,' maybe I knew he was insuperably bound to her. Maybe I thought it was part of the psychological self-mortification I knew he secretly engaged in. Maybe she was part of the way he punished himself for the shortcomings he could not otherwise admit and would not change. He drank too much, she called him a drunk and told him he had to stop drinking or she would leave him, he continued to drink, she stayed.

I do not know if he loved her. He must, I told myself, otherwise he would leave her. He must not, I told myself, or he would not be cheating on her.

I do not know if he loved me. He must, I told myself, look at the way he looks at me. He must not, I told myself, or why would he say the terrible things he says to me? Looking back on it now, with whatever wisdom and perspective I have managed to gain in the intervening years, I think he did love me, though I may be fooling myself. If he did, though, that is the most self-destructive part of our relationship. To love me and choose not to be with me. To make us both suffer. And yet I was choosing suffering by staying with him because of my own demons. The fact that I am still thinking about this and trying to process it shows, too, that I am still trying to escape shame and gain affirmation.

I wish I could remember exactly what precipitated the argument that led to our breakup. I know it was not too long after he called me a bitch and told me to shut my mouth. I know the anger was still fresh within me. I think we had not been able to be together for some time, and I think I was saying I missed him, and I think he was complaining about his wife, and I think I asked him, for the first and only time in our relationship, why he stayed with her if he hated her so much. But I do remember that when I said that, he called me a vulture. He said I hovered over troubled relationships, waiting for them to fall apart so I could pick the bones. He said he needed space.

"Get off me!" he yelled.

I have a very long fuse—I will put up with a lot and continue to assume goodwill—but when I lose my temper, I lose it utterly. Quietly. And irrevocably. Once I have reached the point where I break with a person, it is nearly impossible for them to find a way back.

"You want me to get off you?" I said. "Okay, then."

I hung up the phone and did not speak to him for two years. He called me frantically for days afterward, and I neither answered the phone nor listened to the messages. A few days later, a mutual friend, one of the few people who knew about the affair, told me that Noble had gone to an AA meeting, his very first, and that he had begged the friend to convince me to call him.

"Don't cut him off," my friend said. "Break up with him, okay, he can be a real asshole, but don't cut him out of your life completely. He's all torn up over you."

I shook my head.

"This is the only way I can do it," I said. "If I talk to him, I'll be back with him in a week, and I just can't do it anymore."

I sent Noble a letter through this friend, explaining that I simply could not see him anymore, that it had been wrong in the first place, that he was right, I should not be dating a married man. We were also completely mismatched, we disagreed about everything, and he needed to focus on his sobriety anyway, so the last thing he needed was a messy relationship in the midst of that. That night, presumably after receiving my letter, he called and left a rambling message on my answering machine that whipsawed between begging me not to end it and telling me what a despicable creature I was. I don't remember all of it, but I do recall him commenting on the fact that I had mentioned he was an alcoholic in recovery.

"And you're just loving that, aren't you?" he sneered into the machine.

I was surprised at the remark because I had tiptoed around his drinking for the entirety of our relationship. This was, in fact, the first time I had ever mentioned it. I realized the self-loathing that lay behind the remark, and I realized that I had stayed with him because I felt I could only attract somebody who didn't respect himself and thus would only date somebody he felt

241

was on his level, which is to say, someone else unworthy of respect.

Noble called me nearly every week for the next two years, always late at night, one, two, three o'clock in the morning—drunk, of course, as his slurred voice on my voicemail demonstrated—and always I did not answer. One night—I had moved to Tybee Island by this time—my cell phone rang at two in the morning. I looked at the caller ID. It was Noble. It was a brand new cell phone, issued to me by the newspaper I had begun working for in Savannah, and I didn't know how he had even got the number. I knew our mutual friends would not have given it to him. They knew he was bad for me and didn't want me to get back with him. I don't know why I answered it. Maybe I thought enough time had gone by. Maybe I missed him. I had just broken up with another man I had been dating on and off for a few months. Maybe I was lonely. I put my finger on the green button and pressed it.

"Hey," I said.

"Well, hey to you," he said.

It was as though no time at all had gone by.

"You answered," he said.

"I did."

"I'm glad," he said.

We both sat silently for a moment, I guess taking in the fact that we were back in each other's lives, though to what extent was yet unclear.

"I been seeing you on the television there," he said.

He was referring to the Monday night news broadcast I did on the local ABC News affiliate, with which my current newspaper had a partnership.

"You do a great job," he said. "And you look beautiful. Too much makeup, though. You don't need none of that."

"Well, the makeup artist puts it on," I said. "There's not really much I can do about it."

We talked for a long time, and then I looked at the clock and saw that it was four a.m., so I told him I had to get off the phone because I had to get up for work in a few hours.

"Can I see you on Saturday?" he asked.

I knew I could not see him, because if I did, we would start right back in again. I knew he was no good for me. I knew it would never work.

"Yes," I said.

And the night after next, Saturday night, he drove out to Tybee and took me to dinner at a local seafood place where you sit outside on a wooden deck beneath live oaks and eat Lowcountry Boil and crabs and lobster. As the host seated us, he ordered a bourbon. After dinner we drove to the pier and walked to the end and sat on the bench for a while and talked. Then we went home and went to bed.

"I love you," he said as he lay with me.

"Don't say that," I said. "It's not true."

"It is true."

"Even if it is," I said, "don't say it. Because nothing's ever going to change, so it hurts to hear it. Let's just enjoy this for what it is."

"What can I do to prove it to you?" he said.

"You know what you can do," I said.

"Well, yeah," he said.

He never did it, of course. He never left her, as I knew he would not.

We continued on in that way for another year. He was mellower now, didn't insult me the way he used to, didn't go into fits of bluster and rage. But the well had been poisoned.

The following December I left Georgia for a job in New York's Hudson Valley.

"Call me when you get there so I know you're safe," he said.

"I will," I said.

He was silent on the phone for a minute.

"I do love you," he said.

"I know," I said.

"Bye, angel." And he hung up the phone.

I knew it would be over after that, by default, that he would start up with a new woman. We spoke occasionally on the phone—I called him once while I was stuck in traffic on my way home from work, I don't know why, new town, maybe, still looking for connections, and told him it was his responsibility to entertain me until the cars began moving again, and he did—until one day I called him.

"It's me," I said.

"Hello, angel," he said.

We talked for a minute, and then he said, "Well, we can talk more when you get here. I got to tend to the stew I got going for you."

He thought I was somebody else. After all these years he didn't even recognize my voice. He thought I was another woman.

"Oh," I said. "I can see you thought I was somebody else, so I'll let you go now and get ready for whoever this new woman is you're waiting on."

And I hung up. I realized I had no right to be angry, or to feel jealous, but I was. Even as I knew how ridiculous that was, I

245

was jealous of the new woman with whom he was cheating on his wife.

I didn't hear from him for a few weeks, and then one evening he called. I let the phone go to voicemail. When the message light lit up, I pressed the button and listened. There was a long pause, and a clinking of ice in a glass, and then the rich baritone sound of Noble clearing his throat.

"Hey," he said finally.

He paused again, and then hung up.

I don't know what I was supposed to do with that. I supposed it was Noble testing the waters. I was expected to either call him back if I had gotten over it or let it go if not.

I let it go. I never spoke to him again. He messaged me on Facebook a few times, trying to make small talk, pique my interest in local gossip. I ignored them all.

I visited Savannah about a year after I had moved and did not contact Noble, and I stepped out into Chippewa Square on my arrival hoping desperately not to be seen by somebody who would alert him to my presence. But of course, not five minutes after I set foot on Savannah soil, I bumped into a mutual friend. We talked for a few minutes and then went our separate ways. That evening, when I checked Facebook, I had a message from Noble.

"Davis Williams and 213 other Savannahians told me they experienced a Christian Livermore sighting today. I should hope to believe that you are here, and further that you would call me."

I did not answer, and I left town without calling.

During a subsequent visit I was spotted again, and the intel was again related to Noble.

"Alas, you have returned," he wrote on Messenger that day. "How long will you be here? I would love to see you."

Alas. As though, what? I had been bad for him? He knew he was bad for me?

A few months before I was to leave for Scotland to begin graduate studies at the University of St Andrews, I received another message from Noble, shocking and completely unlike him in its honesty.

"I miss you, Christian. I really do. God help me, I really do miss you. I know that's not much of an appeal, but I can't help it. I don't want to think that I'll never see you again. I know you always had more love and respect for me in your little finger than any other person in this world. I was always too much of a coward to act on it. I want to see you again. Is that possible?"

I was rocked on my heels, and realized that, despite what I had been telling myself, I still loved him. I put the cursor in the message box and answered him for the first time in years.

"I miss you, too," I wrote back. "Of course I do. I don't know how it would be possible to see each other again since I'm leaving for Scotland in a few months, but if I come down there for a visit before I go, I will let you know. Love always, Me."

I wrote this knowing that I would be in Savannah a week before departing for the United Kingdom, and knowing that I would not contact him while I was there. And I did not. I didn't write the message to be false. Maybe I was momentarily weakened by finally hearing the real intimacy I had wanted for so many years to hear, or maybe I needed to say aloud what I had been keeping inside: that no matter how badly he had treated me, I still loved him. Or maybe I wanted to hurt him the way he had hurt me. Maybe I was counting on somebody seeing me while I was there and telling him, so that he would know that I had been there and had not gotten in touch as I promised I would. Maybe I was hoping that would make him see that I was better. Maybe I was hoping to convince myself that I was better.

He messaged me a few times after I moved to Scotland, at first back to his attempts at casual banter. One message read only, "You there?" "Yep," I replied, and that was that. He wrote to me one more time. I did not respond.

One month later, I saw a comment from a mutual friend on Facebook asking if anybody had heard from Noble, that he had crashed his car the night before and the friend couldn't reach him. I began scrolling and surfing and looking for more information. It was true. Noble had driven into a tree on Old Louisville Road. And nobody would ever reach him again.

I had terrible dreams for weeks afterwards. I was kneeling beside his grave. It was open and the coffin above ground. I lifted the coffin lid and he lay there, the decomposition process underway, putrefaction swelling his limbs, fluids leaking from

248

orifices and burst openings in his skin. *"John Brown's Body lies a-mouldering in the grave."* I didn't have these dreams when Deacon died. I still have them sometimes. Often waking dreams, a flash as I sit at my desk, on the couch. I see Noble lying in his coffin, his worm-eaten face half-gone, the cavity where his nose had been open to the light. I don't know why I have these dreams, or what they mean. Something about his body, my failure to possess it, possess it as a thing I could touch and love whenever I wanted and know that it would possess me back, and that now I never would. Or maybe it is simply the violence of a death by car crash, what it must have done to that body I touched so many times, so shocking that my mind is trying to matrix it into something I can understand. I do not know.

Strange things happened afterwards, too. Witchy things. Odd coincidences. A few days after Noble died, I went to change the cover photo on my Facebook page, and I clicked on one of my favorites: A photo of Bonaventure Cemetery in Savannah. As the photo went live, I noticed a comment Noble had made not long before his death that I hadn't noticed at the time: "There's a place waiting for me there, just down that road, where I will sleep in peace forever with my family." A few days after that I went to our Messenger conversation. I don't know why I did it. I guess I just wanted to pretend he was still alive for a moment. The last message he ever sent to me appeared on the screen. He sent it a month before he died: "You are the last woman I touched."

In truth, I know that these are exactly what I said: coincidences, nothing more. But when I think about them, part of me still imagines that they are Noble reaching out to me from wherever he is. I know this is not possible. And yet I entertain the thought.

There have been men before and after Noble and Deacon, obviously. One, though I dated him for nearly five years, is a blur of drinking and sex (with him doing most of the drinking; I have never been much of a drinker). I don't remember us doing much else. Nearly thirty years later, I opened the morning issue of *The Guardian* newspaper on my laptop and saw a photo of him taken on the U.S. Capitol steps during the attempted insurrection. My best friend looked at the photo and shook his head.

"You sure can pick 'em," he said.

I sure can.

I think that of all these damaged men I have been in relationships with, it is Noble I loved the most. If I'm honest, I love him still. How I can love someone who treated me so badly, who had so little respect for my opinions, my beliefs, and my feelings, I do not know. I can only assume it is a product of the fundamental lack of respect I was taught to have for myself as a child growing up in poverty. I think it is because he reproduced most precisely the chaos of my childhood and came the closest to making me feel like the poor white trash I have felt like my whole life. And because he was most like my mother, the love he withheld the most like that I felt I never received from her, his addictions and illnesses the most like hers, his personality as outsized and boisterous.

When I say I loved him the most, I am speaking of *amour fou*, mad love, an untamable or obsessive passion over which one has no control. My first love has been my best friend for thirty-four years, and because that love was not mad and was based on mutual respect, when it ended, we were able to turn it into friendship. Indeed, we have worked very, very hard to turn it into an unshakeable kinship. He is my ride or die, and I am his.

It was different with Noble. Is different. I still feel the love, and I think of good times we had together, but I think more often of the bad times, of the terrible things he said to me, and I ruminate on what it was in me that allowed that. I know the answer. It is the shame of poverty that I continue to drag behind me everywhere I go. But there is another question to which I do not know the answer: How do I make it stop?

The only solution I have come up with so far is to take a break from men for the time being. Because I am not better. Not completely. I am, as my best friend's 100-year-old Irish aunt used to say, better but by no means well. I continue to make the same mistake. For the past ten years I have been in love with a married man. This time he's only about ten years older than me, so I suppose I am improving, but I have repeated the same pattern yet again. With one difference. This time I have chosen not to act on my feelings, not to even make him aware of them. And I count that as something. Because I could have him if I wanted. I know I could. I see it by the way he looks at me.

I don't want to do that to him, or to his wife. Unlike Noble, he is a good man, and I want him to be happy. I have dated several men during this time, but for whatever reason, probably because I intentionally chose men who would not hold my interest so that I could continue to focus on this man, the relationships have gone nowhere. So, rather than make my feelings known to the married man I am in love with, I choose to be alone. And I count that as progress.

When I wake up these days, I have to sit on the edge of my bed and massage my knees for a few minutes, otherwise they won't work, and sometimes my right hip starts to give way as I walk and I have to grab onto something so I don't fall. I am waiting for test results that will determine whether I need the hip replaced immediately or if it can wait a little longer.

Still, I thought one day not long ago, all in all, things were immeasurably better. I had finally got the passport. I had to miss a month's rent payment and bills to pay the cost of document translations, processing fees and apostilles, and it took me nearly a year to get caught up, but I did it. I had the passport I needed for the jobs I was being considered for. I had a book coming out. Finally, I thought, maybe things will be okay.

Then, one morning, while I was brushing my teeth, I felt something loose in my mouth. I thought it was a piece of the apple I had just eaten. My teeth are straight and white, because in America they put fluoride in the drinking water, but the severe gum disease from a childhood without adequate dental care and a lifetime of sporadic dental insurance has left me with little pockets between my teeth and gums where the enamel has eroded. Like America, my teeth look shiny and clean, but they are rotting on the inside.

I rinsed and spit, and something white clattered into the sink. I picked it up. It was not a piece of apple. It was a tooth. I threw it in the waste bin and covered it with toilet paper. Then I returned to the kitchen table where I had been sitting with a very old friend and tried to pretend it hadn't happened. He couldn't see it. Strangely, the tooth was a molar, the gap it left in the back of my mouth hidden just behind the spot where my lips part in smiling, as if my very body was conspiring to hide my shame.

But he could tell I was shaken, and he asked me what was wrong. Oh, I was just thinking about something that happened when I was a kid, I told him. He asked me what and I said there was no point in talking about it. He knew all about it, this friend of nearly thirty-five years, all about my childhood, had heard all the stories, and he knew that simply telling him I was thinking about my childhood was sometimes enough for me.

"At least it's over now," he said. "At least you're done with all that now."

I laughed bitterly and thought of the tooth. It would be taken out with the trash, but the memory of it, like my childhood, is lodged in my throat.

END

ABOUT THE AUTHOR

Christian is also the author of a fiction chapbook, *Girl, Lost and Found* (Alien Buddha Press, 2021), and her stories and essays have appeared in anthologies and literary journals including *Santa Fe Writers Project*, *Salt Hill Journal*, *The Texas Review*, *Meat for Tea*, and *Witch-Pricker*. She has a PhD in Creative Writing from the University of St Andrews in Scotland with an academic focus on medieval English literature and has taught creative writing at Newcastle University and medieval literature at the University of St Andrews. She worked for ten years as a journalist.

Indie

Blu(e)

Indie Blu(e) Publishing is a progressive, feminist micro-press, committed to producing honest and thought-provoking works. Our anthologies are meant to celebrate diversity and raise awareness. The editors all passionately advocate for human rights; mental health awareness; chronic illness awareness; sexual abuse survivors; and LGBTQ+ equality. It is our mission, and a great honor, to provide platforms for those voices that are stifled and stigmatized.

Hospital Poems

Nancy Dunlop

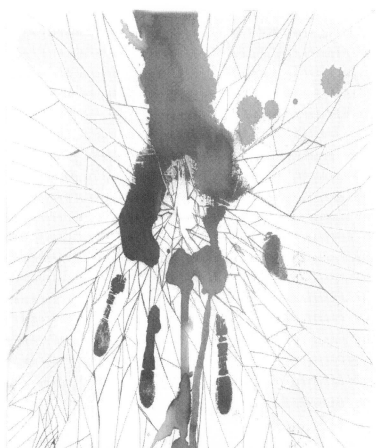

THROUGH THE LOOKING GLASS
REFLECTING ON MADNESS AND CHAOS WITHIN

An Indie Blu(e) Publishing Anthology

BUT YOU DON'T
LOOK SICK

The Real Life Adventures of Fibro Bitches, Lupus Warriors,
and other Superheroes Battling Invisible Illness

An Indie Blu(e) Publishing Anthology

WE WILL NOT BE SILENCED

The Lived Experience of Sexual Harassment and Sexual Assault Told Powerfully Through Poetry, Prose, Essay, and Art